P9-DDX-256

THE THRESHOLD OF CHRISTIANITY

Between the Testaments

WESTMINSTER GUIDES TO THE BIBLE

Edwin M. Good, General Editor

THE THRESHOLD OF CHRISTIANITY

Between the Testaments

by
LAWRENCE E. TOOMBS

Philadelphia
THE WESTMINSTER PRESS

LIBRARY OF CONGRESS CATALOG CARD NO. 60-5226

PRINTED IN THE UNITED STATES OF AMERICA

Contents

Preface

SINCE the finding of the Dead Sea scrolls in 1947, the realization has dawned on many people that more was going on in the two centuries before the rise of Christianity than they had dreamed. As a matter of fact, a tremendous amount of hard thinking and faithful living was taking place in those two hundred " silent years."

In this book we are introduced to this fascinating period " between the Testaments," to the faith of heroes and martyrs, to the high wisdom of sages and scholars, to the weird visions of seers caught up in God's glory and the urgency of their times, to the fears, the hopes, the delights of men common and uncommon. The years were anything but " silent "; they resound with the voices of God's people. We see where Israel went in the years beyond those which the Old Testament tells us about. And we see the brilliant background against which Jesus and the New Testament writers lived and thought.

If this book does nothing else for the reader, it should throw glowing light on innumerable New Testament passages for him. But we may suspect it will do more. It will open new depths in his own thinking, depths that take him, as they took those long-dead, faithful Jews, to the very heart of the most profound issues of faith.

The Westminster Guides to the Bible grew in the first instance out of the stimulus of the Layman's Theological Library. If, we thought, laymen in the church could be so eloquently encouraged to be theologians, why could they not be encouraged to be Biblical scholars as well? In the modern resurgence of serious thinking about the Christian faith, Bible study has played a major role. But the methods and results of this recent study have not been made available to laymen.

The Westminster Guides to the Bible seek to fill this gap. In nine brief volumes, we introduce the riches of the major portions of the Bible and of the period "between the Testaments." The writers share the conviction that the Bible lies at the heart of Christianity, and that it is imperative that laymen be aided to take a firm grip on Biblical faith. We are certain that this means no denial of the mind. On the contrary, the Bible demands the utmost our minds can give it, and searching study repays our efforts with new insights.

Of course, we are primarily concerned with the Bible, not with our books about it. We hope that the reader will have his Bible in hand as he reads these books, and that he will turn to it again when he has finished. We dare to hope that he will turn from these guides with greater anticipation to the Bible itself.

And it is with laymen, who are the backbone of the church, that we are concerned. We have written, not for scholars already learned, but for those who seek to learn. We are certain that no wishy-washy faith, no cheap "religiousness," is wanted. In the vigor of Biblical faith we trust that the reader will find invigoration. If so, the church of Christ will be served.

EDWIN M. GOOD

Chapter 1 | *Books and Men*

The Incomplete Old Testament

The Old Testament resembles an unfinished symphony. Like a symphony, it has its great themes: the Covenant, the deeds of God by which he delivered his people from slavery, the repeated rebellion and return of Israel. But in the end these themes are left hanging in the air, unresolved and incomplete. The Old Testament history ends with Nehemiah enforcing a national reformation the results of which we never learn, and the last words of The Book of Nehemiah are a forward-looking prayer, "Remember me, O my God, for good." Surely, the reader says, there must be something more than this.

The prophetic movement, which blazed with inspiration in Amos, Hosea, and Isaiah, fizzles out like a wet firecracker in stock phrases and trivialities. Even in its heyday, prophetic teaching looked beyond itself for a fulfillment in "the days to come." The poetic sections of the Old Testament are haunted by the same sense of incompleteness. Job wrestles with the meaning of human suffering, and does not answer his own questions. The writer of Ecclesiastes investigates the meaning of life, only to become sour and negative in his conclusions. The psalms are full of unfulfilled longings, and their writers usually lived with one eye on the future. The Old Testament was clearly "to be continued."

The Unpredictable New Testament

During the last week of Jesus' life, as Mark records it, his opponents engaged him in five vigorous debates with a view to exposing him as a false teacher. (Mark, chs. 11 to 13.) Neither the questions raised nor the groups that raised them would have been predicted on the basis of the Old Testament. The Sadducees, Pharisees, Herodians, and lawyers, who question Jesus, are unknown in the Old Testament. Where did they come from? The question of the authority of John's baptism (ch. 11:27-33) is a question about an institution not found in Old Testament law. "Is it lawful to pay taxes to Caesar or not?" (ch. 12:13-17) is unprepared for in the Old Testament, where there is no Caesar. The Old Testament contains a few scattered references to the resurrection of the dead (notably Isa., chs. 24 to 27; Dan. 12:1-4), but who would have predicted that it would become important enough to divide Judaism into two parties (Mark 12:18; Acts 23:6-10)? The problem of which is the greatest commandment (Mark 12:28-34) reflects a good deal of thinking on the relative value of the various laws, and such thought is not characteristic of the Old Testament. Jesus' teaching on "the last days" (ch. 13) presupposes considerable speculation about the end of history for which the Old Testament does not prepare us. Paul preaches to Jews in a dozen pagan cities. How did they get there?

The two Testaments, bound together in our Bible, are like a serial story of which the next-to-last installment is lost, or like an amnesia victim who has forgotten the events of one crucial year of his life. Between the Old Testament and the New about two hundred years went by, crowded with swiftly moving history, hard thinking, and much writing. The events, the books, and the men that filled the inter-Testamental period are the subject of this book. To get a complete picture we must begin with the rise of Alexander the Great (333 B.C.) and end with the second Jewish revolt against Rome (A.D. 135): a matter of 468 years. We must consider not only the Jews in Palestine but those living away from the homeland in the great Gentile cities. And there are about sixty important books that come out of the period, including the Biblical book of Daniel and the controversial Dead Sea scrolls. The age, the people, and the books are important because they take us from the Old Testament to the threshold of Christianity.

The Hidden Books

The favorite Sunday evening pastime in my childhood home, where weekday activities were forbidden on the Sabbath, was turning over the pages of the huge family Bible and looking at the amazing pictures of ancient cities, coins, gods, kings, and heroes to be found there. One of these boyhood explorations brought me face to face with a new word: "Apocrypha." This jawbreaker was the heading of a series of fifteen books, printed between the Old and New Testaments. The titles of these books also had a mysterious quality:

- I and II Esdras
- Tobit
- Judith
- Additions to Esther
- The Wisdom of Solomon
- Ecclesiasticus, or The Wisdom of Jesus the Son of Sirach
- Baruch
- The Letter of Jeremiah
- The Prayer of Azariah and the Song of the Three Young Men
- Susanna
- Bel and the Dragon
- The Prayer of Manasseh
- I and II Maccabees

I had never seen these books in any other Bible, nor heard them read in church. Why were they in the " big " Bible and not in the " ordinary " Bible, and what were they doing " between the Testaments "? I found out the answers to these questions in due time.

The name Apocrypha (a Greek word meaning " hidden ") was given to these books, not because they were ever lost, but because they were believed to contain mysterious teachings the significance of which was " hidden " from the ordinary reader. The story of the Apocrypha goes back to Jewish communities living in Egypt in the third century before Christ. Their scriptures (most of the Old Testament) were in Hebrew, but they spoke Greek. And though they had a variety of partial Greek translations, there was no standard version. Under Ptolemy II, King of Egypt (285-246 B.C.), work began on an official translation of the Torah. The task was expanded and continued over several centuries until all the sacred books, including the Apocrypha, were available in good Greek versions. The Greek Bible received the name Septuagint (the word means " seventy ") from the tradition that the original translation committee had consisted of seventy members. It was a godsend to the early Christian church. In its pages Gentile Christians could read in their own language the story of God's dealing with Israel. The church eagerly adopted the Septuagint, and by doing so inherited the Apocrypha, which is still an integral part of the Roman Catholic Bible.

The Hebrew Bible does not contain the Apocrypha because, after considerable debate, the Jewish rabbis decided that the books of the Apocrypha should not be regarded as sacred. This decision was made final about A.D. 100. At the Protestant Reformation, Luther, Calvin, and the other Reformers returned to the Hebrew Bible and excluded the Apocrypha. They regarded its books as of no force in establishing doctrines, but as valuable " for the advancement and furtherance of the knowledge of the history, and for the instruction of godly manners " (The Geneva Bible, 1560). To symbolize the special place of the Apocrypha, the books were separated from the rest of the Bible and put between the Testaments. This is not at all a bad position for them, because they are among the most important literary products of the inter-Testamental period.

The best sellers of this period were adventure stories, such as Tobit and Judith. Tobit, a God-fearing man, became blind as a result of an act of compassion. His son, Tobias, journeyed to Media on a mission for his father with the angel Raphael as traveling companion. In Media he rescued a beautiful woman from her murderous demon lover. Returning home with the gall of a fish obtained earlier through Raphael's help, he anointed his father's eyes with it, thus curing his blindness. Judith is an ancient forerunner of the spy story. An Assyrian general, Holofernes, had Bethulia under siege, and its garrison, desperate with thirst, was on the point of surrender. A charming and pious widow, Judith, slipped into the enemy camp, won the confidence of Holofernes, and beheaded him while he was helplessly drunk.

The Apocrypha contains several additions to Old Testament books: three to Daniel, six to Esther, and one each to Jeremiah and II Chronicles. Two of the Daniel additions are sometimes published in collections of detective stories as the earliest-known whodunits. In Susanna, Daniel rescues a woman accused of adultery by proving that two leading citizens were framing her for the crime, and in Bel and the Dragon he exposes the trickery of the Babylonian priesthood. The third supplement to Daniel, The Prayer of Azariah and the Song of the Three Young Men, contains the worship offered by Shadrach, Meshach, and Abednego from within the fiery furnace. The Letter of Jeremiah, an attack on idolatry, is supposed to have been written by Jeremiah, the prophet, to the exiles in Babylon. Second Chronicles 33:10-13 says that, while the wicked king Manasseh was a prisoner in Babylon "he entreated the favor of the Lord his God and humbled himself greatly before the God of his fathers." A deeply moving confession of sin and plea for forgiveness is attributed to the king in The Prayer of Manasseh. Baruch is not properly an addition to a Biblical book. It purports to have been written by Jeremiah's scribe, Baruch, to the Babylonian exiles to encourage them and tell them what they ought to do.

The two books of Esdras are as different as night and day. First Esdras merely repeats most of Ezra and Nehemiah. Its one novel feature is a debate among three of the Persian king's guardsmen on the subject, "What is the strongest thing in the world?" A case is made for wine, the king, and women, but the audience agrees that "Great is truth, and strongest of all!" Second Esdras belongs to the type of mysterious and symbolic literature called "apocalyptic," which deals with the end of the present age. It stands between Daniel in the Old Testament and Revelation in the New, and casts much light on Jewish speculation about the last things.

The Apocrypha is heir to the Old Testament's intense interest in the history of the people of God. The two books of Maccabees tell the story of the victorious Jewish revolt against tyrannical Greek overlords. First Maccabees is an accurate and thrilling history of the war; II Maccabees is disorganized and fanciful. A second Old Testament literary type found also in the Apocrypha is the wisdom literature. Centered in the problems of everyday life, and enthusiastic in their praise of wisdom, The Wisdom of Solomon and Ecclesiasticus continue the tradition of the wise men of Israel who produced Proverbs, Ecclesiastes, and Job.

The Outside Books

A rival in size to the family Bible is R. H. Charles's two-volume work, *The Apocrypha and Pseudepigrapha of the Old Testament* (Oxford University Press, 1913). The desk groans under its 1,554 pages. We have dealt briefly with the Apocryphal books. The Pseudepigrapha, however, is another and more difficult matter. The name means "false titles" and comes from the practice of its real authors of claiming that their books were written by famous Biblical men, such as Solomon, Enoch, Baruch, Abraham, and Moses. The Pseudepigrapha is such a hodgepodge of miscellaneous writings, dating anywhere from 200 B.C. to A.D. 100, that any statement made about it is more than half wrong.

Part of the difficulty is that the books of the Pseudepigrapha were gathered into one collection in only relatively modern times. As we have seen, the Apocrypha was never concealed, but was always available along with the books of the Bible. The Pseudepigrapha enjoyed no such protection. Its books were circulated separately, and outside the sacred collection, and were much more likely to meet with unfortunate accidents. It is not uncommon to find in the Pseudepigrapha an early Jewish writing overlaid by later Jewish and Christian additions. In some cases the text in its original language has been lost, and we must make do with an Ethiopic, a Slavonic, or a Syriac translation.

Admittedly, this is not a satisfactory state of affairs, but the Pseudepigrapha is so important for an understanding of New Testament Christianity that something must be done with it. A description of the main themes and a passing mention of the more important books is all that is possible here. The reader is assured that the Pseudepigrapha has not been ignored in preparing the last three chapters of this book. If he remains unsatisfied (as he should), he can always flee to the arms of R. H. Charles.

The Pseudepigrapha makes long additions of an obviously legendary kind to the Old Testament narratives. Examples of this are The Martyrdom of Isaiah, The Lives of the Prophets, and the life of Adam and Eve (miscalled The Apocalypse of Moses). Israel's history is a major interest, but attention is focused on the beginning and the end. Indeed, " the last things " (eschatology) are almost an obsession with the writers (see especially Enoch and The Apocalypse of Baruch). The Messiah, the resurrection, and the Last Judgment are recurring themes, clothed in visionary language that is apt to make the modern reader feel either confused or impatient. The religious problems that claim most attention are the doctrines of God and of the angels, good and bad, the law, sin and forgiveness, free will and predestination, good works and justification — themes that the New Testament shares. Some of the books attempt to recommend the Jewish faith to the Gentile world (The Sibylline Oracles, III Maccabees), whereas others are indebted to pagan thought for some of their ideas (IV Maccabees, Slavonic Enoch, The Testament of Abraham). The Testaments of the Twelve Patriarchs has the universalistic doctrine that all the Gentiles will in the end be saved, and The Psalms of Solomon continue in a stilted way the poetic tradition of the Hebrew psalms, revealing the depth of personal religion in the period.

A Philosopher and a Soldier

Of other books bearing on the inter-Testamental period, the philosophical writings of Philo Judaeus and the histories of Flavius Josephus are particularly important.

Philo lived in Alexandria in Egypt between the years 20 B.C. and A.D. 54. He was, therefore, a contemporary of Jesus, but his world was very different from that of the carpenter of Nazareth. The metropolis of Alexandria, one of the intellectual centers of the Greek world, was a place of libraries, universities, and philosophical debates. The philosophers claimed to have a grasp on truth, but to the Jew truth was expressed in the divinely revealed law. It should be possible, then, to harmonize the Scriptures and the best thought of the philosophers. To this task Philo dedicated himself. He held that God is eternal being, uncontaminated by matter. Man is a soul bound to a material body, and to be saved is to be released from the material and to be drawn upward to God. The intermediary between God and man is the Son of God, the divine Logos or Word. (Compare John, ch. 1.) In his study of the Scriptures, Philo looked for a deeper meaning than appeared on the surface of the text and made use of symbols and allegories to discover it.

Philo does us the service of showing how Jews outside Palestine attempted to express their faith in ways that the Gentile world would understand. It was to such communities that the first Christian missionaries went. Students of the New Testament trace the influence of Philo in several New Testament books, notably John's Gospel and Hebrews.

Flavius Josephus (A.D. 35–95) was a well-educated, well-traveled Palestinian Jew. During the first revolt against Rome (A.D. 66–70) he commanded an army in Galilee, but after a siege of forty-seven days he surrendered to the Roman captain, Vespasian. He predicted that his conqueror would become emperor, and when the prediction came true Josephus was rewarded with Roman citizenship, a pension, and an estate. He then began a literary career devoted to interpreting the Jew to the Roman. Writing in Greek, he composed two histories: *The Jewish War* and *The Antiquities of the Jews.* The first is an accurate record of the revolt, in which Josephus himself took part. The second paints a broader canvas—the whole sweep of Jewish history from the Creation to the war with Rome. The Bible is the main source for the early chapters, but after Alexander the Great, Josephus is on his own. Although he slants his work to the Roman reader and presents the Jews in as favorable a light as possible, Josephus is a conscientious workman, and his history gives us the basic account of the history and institutions of his people on the threshold of Christianity.

The Dead Sea Scrolls

A totally unexpected addition to inter-Testamental literature came with the discovery in 1947 and in subsequent years of the amazing Dead Sea scrolls. A Jordanian shepherd boy began the excitement by the chance find of seven ancient manuscripts in a cave at the northwest end of the Dead Sea. Numerous smaller pieces of manuscript were later taken from the same cave. All the evidence indicated that the bulk of the documents was written between 100 B.C. and A.D. 70, and had remained hidden in the dry cave for almost two thousand years. No one had believed it possible that Biblical and non-Biblical books of such antiquity would be recovered in Palestine. Enthusiasm ran high, and the discovery was called "unprecedented," "fabulous," and "fantastic."

The tireless Bedouin rummaged through cave after cave, and a team of archaeologists joined the search. The number of manuscript-bearing caves increased from Cave I to Cave XI. In Cave III the mysterious copper scrolls were found. Cave IV yielded thousands of manuscript fragments. Cave XI produced two nearly complete and five fragmentary scrolls. Such a large concentration of books in one neighborhood suggested the library of a fairly large community. The buildings belonging to such a group were found on a nearby plateau and excavated.

Gradually the picture emerged of a semimonastic, extremely bookish Jewish sect living in the wilderness by the Dead Sea in the period from about 135 B.C. to A.D. 68. The accidents of history and geography have preserved for us an intimate picture of their life and thought, at which we will look in detail in Chapter 4.

The Dead Sea sect possessed copies of every book of the Old Testament with the possible exception of Esther, but the most popular were The Prophets, The Psalms, and Deuteronomy. They also studied at least some of the apocryphal and pseudepigraphic writings. What shed most light on the inter-Testamental period, however, are the new books that were unknown before the discovery of the Dead Sea scrolls.

The sect that produced the scrolls lived under the Old Testament law. Detailed regulations and elaborate legal theory, designed to control life in the present age and in the age to come, were set down in a class of books called "Rules" or "Manuals." The working laws for the day-to-day life of the community were contained in a seven-foot leather scroll: The Manual of Discipline, or Rule of the Community. This document gives regulations for admission to the sect, its philosophy of the struggle between good and evil in the soul of man, and the general laws of community life. Two columns, bearing the title "Rule of the Congregation," were attached to the beginning of the Manual. Here the sect had sketched the laws that would govern united and restored Israel in the future Kingdom of the Messiah. The third "Rule" scroll, "The War of the Sons of Light with the Sons of Darkness," is the battle plan for the war to end wars, the final battle between Israel and the evil powers that would come against her at the end of history.

A book with a romantic history, The Damascus Document, is related to the three "Rules." The document gets its name from the fact that it contains rules for the guidance of a Jewish sect said to be living in " camps " in the land of Damascus. A fuller form of the title might well be " The Document of the Damascus Covenanters." It was discovered in 1910 in a storeroom for worn-out manuscripts attached to a Cairo synagogue. The two fragmentary manuscripts of this book appeared to be medieval copies of an ancient document, but the mysterious sentences, peculiar interpretations of Scripture, and obscure historical references did not fit closely with any other known piece of Jewish literature. The striking similarity between The Damascus Document and the Dead Sea scrolls, both in the way it treated history and in its legal sections, was quickly noted. The discovery of fragments of this very document in Cave IV confirmed beyond doubt that The Damascus Document belonged to the Dead Sea sect.

A Biblically centered sect would be expected to write commentaries on the Old Testament books. The fragments from Caves I and IV included parts of commentaries on Hosea, Isaiah, Nahum, Micah, Zephaniah, and The Psalms, and Cave I yielded a nearly complete commentary on Habakkuk. Since the sect interpreted the words of the prophets as applying to its own history and times, these commentaries are invaluable sources of information about its life and thought.

Some of the sect's books remind us of the Apocrypha and Pseudepigrapha. There is an Aramaic version of Genesis, which has many additions to the accepted Biblical text. A large scroll contains a collection of thanksgiving hymns, modeled after the Biblical psalms, and reminding one of the psalms of Solomon. Scrolls dealing with astrology and the calendar are reminiscent of The Book of Jubilees, and reflect typical inter-Testamental interests.

A whole library of literature had already been written about the Dead Sea scrolls. The two books by Millar Burrows, *The*

Dead Sea Scrolls (The Viking Press, Inc., 1955) and *More Light on the Dead Sea Scrolls* (The Viking Press, Inc., 1958), stand out as the most thorough and scholarly treatment of the subject. Two members of the international team charged with the study of the scrolls have told the " inside story " of scroll research: J. M. Allegro, *The Dead Sea Scrolls* (Pelican Publishing Co., 1956), and Frank Moore Cross, Jr., *The Ancient Library of Qumran and Modern Biblical Studies* (Doubleday & Co., Inc., 1958).

A Look Ahead

The reader who has hung on up to this point will appreciate the fact that there is an embarrassment of riches available for the study of the period between the Testaments. Our task is to cut a straight path through the forest of sources that we have been reviewing. Our main interest is in the religious thought stirring within Judaism at this time. And we wish to see how this thought is related to the incomplete Old Testament on the one side, and the unpredictable New Testament on the other. It will be necessary first of all to outline the course of history on the world scene. This is done in Chapter 2. We shall move from there to consider the way in which world events affected Jewish life both in the homeland of Palestine and in the Jewish communities in foreign lands (Chapter 3). The Dead Sea community provides a concrete example of one Jewish group living and thinking in the setting of these events (Chapter 4). The view then widens to include the Apocryphal and Pseudepigraphal literature in general under three headings: " The Present Age " (Chapter 5), " The Age to Come " (Chapter 6), and " Life Under the Law " (Chapter 7). Because of its close relationship to this body of literature The Book of Daniel will come up for consideration at numerous points along the way.

Chapter 2 | *The Changing World*

Alexander and After

After two hundred years of world rule the Persian Empire had, without realizing it, grown old and tired. Like an aging champion, out of condition but still full of confidence, Persia was waiting for a vigorous young challenger to take away her crown. About 340 B.C. that challenger was preparing himself in Macedonia. Philip, a king tough enough to match the ruggedness of his mountain kingdom, had, over the opposition of the orator Demosthenes, forced the Greek cities into unity, and was almost ready for a decisive stroke against Persia when the hand of the assassin reached him, and he died on the eve of his great adventure (336 B.C.).

His son, Alexander, already a seasoned soldier and administrator at the age of twenty, took up his father's task with vigor. Two years were required to consolidate his control over the Greek cities and to prepare the army. Then the heavily armed infantry with its cavalry, light support troops, and siege machines faced toward the east. For the first time in history, Europe moved victoriously into Asia, and the tide of empire flowed from west to east. A left into Asia Minor, culminating in the Battle of Issus, a sweeping right through Phoenicia to occupy Egypt (Palestine and Jerusalem passed under Greek control as an incident in this campaign), and a straight drive to the heart of Persia, ending in the Battle of Gaugamela, near modern Mosul, brought the Persian Empire crashing to defeat. Its last king, Darius III, was murdered by his own followers, and its twenty vast provinces were at the disposal of the conqueror (330 B.C.). Alexander's restless energy carried him on to the mountains of Afghanistan and the river valleys of north India, and to death in 323 B.C. at the age of thirty-two from hard drinking, hard campaigning, malarial fever, and three major battle wounds.

With Alexander dead, leaving no heir, his sprawling conquests could not be held together in political unity. As The Book of Daniel accurately reports, the empire was "broken and divided toward the four winds of heaven" (ch. 11:4). The generals of the army were strong and ambitious men, but none was powerful enough to take Alexander's place, and the story of their feuds and struggles for power is one of the most complicated pages of ancient history. Fortunately for those interested in events in Palestine, the spotlight quickly settles on two prominent figures, Ptolemy I, called Lagi, and Seleucus I, called Nicanor.

Ptolemy had been Alexander's boyhood companion, a fellow student with him under the philosopher Aristotle, and a distinguished commander from the first campaign to the last. Seeing the confused state of the empire after Alexander's death, he withdrew to the rich and easily defensible province of Egypt, and there established a royal line that ran through fourteen members and ended with the famous (or infamous) Cleopatra. Judah was a frontier province of Ptolemy's kingdom, and continued to be ruled from Alexandria for 115 years until 198 B.C. Under the Ptolemies the Jews were heavily taxed, but otherwise were allowed to develop their culture and religion without undue interference. The right to live by their traditional laws was guaranteed, and the Temple enjoyed tax exemption and a certain amount of state support.

In contrast to Ptolemy, Seleucus was a Johnny-come-lately. During Alexander's lifetime he fought his way from relative obscurity to command of the powerful infantry, and during the struggles after Alexander's death, he adroitly carved out a kingdom for himself by intrigue and fighting skill. From his capital at Antioch on the Orontes River he ruled from Babylonia to the northern borders of Syria. His ambitions included control of Palestine, vital to him as a buffer against Egypt, but neither he nor his immediate successors were able to make good this desire. In 198 B.C., however, Antiochus III defeated Ptolemy V, and Palestine came under Seleucid rule. For a short time the Jews enjoyed their old privileges, but soon the conqueror's hand began to press more heavily, and the fires of persecution broke out. With this change in royal policy a new era in Jewish history begins. Before entering upon it we should pause to consider the impact that the new world order made on the Jews.

The reader may like to compare the colorful, visionary account of the events just described in Dan. 8:1-8 with the matter-of-fact summary in I Macc. 1:1-9.

The Impact of the Greeks

Alexander's eastward march was dramatic in more than the military sense. It brought the East, ancient as human history and rich with the wisdom of centuries, into close contact with the restless, inquiring spirit of the Greeks. To fuse these two into a creative unity was the dream of Alexander and the ideological driving force behind his conquests.

In the wake of the armies came merchants, scholars, tourists, and settlers, all speaking Greek, and bringing new ideas in architecture, government, and philosophy. Cities modeled after the Greek pattern sprang up everywhere and became radiating centers of the new culture, outposts of Greece in an alien environment. Out of the ferment a culture was created, neither purely Greek nor purely Oriental, to which the name "Hellenistic" is given. The Romans, who were excellent administrators but rarely cultural innovators, scarcely disturbed the surface of Hellenism in the East, and Hellenistic civilization, therefore, provides the setting for the New Testament. In Jesus' day a league of Greek cities, called "the Decapolis," brought Hellenistic influences to the very borders of Judea. The infant churches, such as those founded by Paul and those mentioned in the book of The Revelation, were islands of Christianity in a sea of Hellenistic city life. Early Christianity had the peculiarly difficult task of mediating to the Hellenistic world a religion that had arisen in the soil of Judaism. The writings of the New Testament and the events in the primitive church can be understood only as one sees the first Christians trying to reach across the gap between Judaism and Hellenism without sacrificing anything essential to their faith.

Between Athens and Jerusalem — the Greek spirit and the Jewish — deep and fundamental tensions existed. The Greek heritage was an easy, tolerant cosmopolitanism, founded on polytheistic religion and on supreme confidence in the human ability to grapple successfully with human problems. The Jewish heritage was an intense faith in one God and one people of God, nationalistic and intolerant, profoundly mistrustful of human abilities when they claimed an absolute validity for themselves.

The distinctively Hebrew genius arose from the *national* covenant, established by God with his people. In spite of the international viewpoint of some of the prophets, the structure of Hebrew thought was radically nationalistic. The Hellenistic spirit was, by contrast, sweepingly cosmopolitan. The citizens of a given city might be proud of their own institutions and accomplishments, but they were sympathetically receptive to other men, other religions, and other ways of life. The large colonies of Jews who lived in each of the Hellenistic cities must have appeared exclusive and narrow to their pagan fellow citizens.

Hellenistic society was as tolerant of gods as of opinions. After Alexander it was customary for Hellenistic rulers to claim divine status in the manner of the god-kings of the East (Dan., ch. 6), and for their subjects to accept this in stride. There were, after all, "many 'gods' and many 'lords'" (I Cor. 8:5), some of them far less reputable than the king. The Jew, however, could maintain his separate community life and fulfill his covenant obligations only by the strictest loyalty to the one God of the covenant. To him, a multiplicity of gods was a religious monstrosity, and a divine king the ultimate blasphemy.

Anyone who has come under the influence of Greek philosophy takes it to be self-evident that the way knowledge is obtained is by the free and uninhibited use of the human mind. The inquiring intellect can be trusted to recognize truth and to reject error. The Jew relied for all knowledge that was really important on the revelation of God to the covenant community, and on the religious tradition that interpreted and preserved the revelation. Any tinkering with the process by the unaided human intellect was a source of error, not of truth.

The contrast in the understanding of the source of knowledge is only a special instance of a fundamental contrast in attitudes toward the means of salvation. Hebrew tradition held that salvation is "not by might, nor by power, but by [God's] Spirit" (Zech. 4:6), and roundly declared, "Cursed is the man who trusts in man" (Jer. 17:5). The Greek was also heir to a tradition: the heroic ideal, stemming from the epics of Homer, and expressed in the character of Alexander. Salvation comes from exceptional men, who strenuously cultivate their mental and physical powers and then risk them hugely and joyfully in some great cause. The Greeks, lovers of beauty and art, enjoyed sports and the theater. The Jews resented both, not because of prudish dislike of publicly displaying the human body, but in protest against the vaunting of merely human powers. The Greek love of beauty for its own sake found no sympathetic response in the Jew, to whom it seemed like skating on the thin ice of pride.

It is clear that the Jew could live at peace in the Hellenistic world only so long as its governments kept their hands off distinctively Jewish institutions and attitudes. If for any reason Hellenistic tolerance broke down, the Jewish spirit became a seed of revolt, the more bloody and tenacious because of the religious issues at stake. Three times in four centuries the Jewish populace took up arms, once against the Greeks and twice against the Romans, until the Roman legions finally crushed the life out of the Jewish state and it could rise no more.

The Revolt of "the Hammerer"

The Book of Daniel has no good word to say for the eighth Seleucid king, Antiochus IV, Epiphanes, who is contemptuously called "the little horn" (ch. 8:9, and see ch. 11:36-39). In justice to Antiochus, his position was not easy. He was under pressure from the Romans on the west and the Parthians on the east, threatened by insurrection at home, and chronically in need of money. The king's answer to his problems was an attempt to unify his kingdom in a common Hellenistic culture and religion. In this program he emphatically included the Jews, whose stubborn faith he regarded as a divisive force on his vulnerable southern frontier.

Antiochus had good reason to hope for success. The Jewish

upper and ruling classes were already badly infiltrated by Hellenism, and a bitter struggle for the important office of high priest was in progress. Jason had replaced the legitimate officeholder, Onias III, by offering Antiochus a handsome bribe and promises to aid in the Hellenizing of the Jews. But a rival candidate, Menelaus, outbid him and took his place. Jason raised an army, and forced Menelaus out of office, until Antiochus brought him back and installed him by force. The people were thus treated to the ugly spectacle of two Jews bargaining and brawling for the high priesthood with a pagan god-king as seller and referee.

When his policies met with opposition, Antiochus turned tyrant. The Temple was looted of its treasures. Jerusalem was burned, stripped of its walls and left defenseless. The daily sacrifices in the Temple were stopped, and an altar to Olympian Zeus, "the abomination that makes desolate" (Dan. 11:31), went up on the altar of burnt offerings. Sabbath observance, the practice of circumcision, and possession of copies of the law were forbidden; the penalty for failure to comply — death!

Mattathias, an elderly priest of the village of Modein, was blessed with a stout heart and five stalwart sons. When called upon to offer a public sacrifice on a heathen altar he ran his sword through the king's officer and fled with his sons to the hills. This family (called the "Hasmonaeans" after an ancestor, Hasmon) became the rallying point for "everyone who offered himself willingly for the law." At first the rebels used the hit-and-run tactics of guerrilla fighters, but when Judas took command at the death of his father (167 B.C.) they were strong enough to put a regular army in the field.

Judas, the third son of Mattathias, was the first real military leader of the Maccabean Revolt. He earned his nickname, Maccabeus, "the Hammerer," in the numerous battles so vividly described in I Maccabees, and was killed in action leading the last desperate charge of a defeated army. The death of Judas (161 B.C.) marked the low point of the revolt, but the diplomacy and victories of two of Judas' brothers, Jonathan and Simon, restored the ground that had been lost. When Simon died, religious and political liberty had been achieved, and the Hasmonaeans' rule had been firmly established over a territory extending from Samaria to the Sinai desert. Simon's successors behaved as Oriental monarchs have done from time immemorial, murdering their opponents, oppressing their subjects, and putting down rebellion with a rod of iron. The long reign of Alexander Jannaeus (102–76 B.C.) saw the greatest expansion of the little Jewish Kingdom. After his time there was a period of decline until the coming of the Romans in 63 B.C.

The Maccabean Revolt is the key event of the period between the Testaments. It resulted in an independent Jewish Kingdom, but, at the same time, it broke up the old, inner religious unity of Israel and left the people of God fragmented into separate, and often hostile, groups. These sects will be considered in detail in the next chapter, but at this point a brief look at the general principles that called them into existence will be useful.

The chief supporters of the revolt in its early days were those devout families which had remained faithful to the law under the stress of foreign rule and foreign culture. To them the persecutions under Antiochus IV seemed to be the last period of trial before God asserted his authority and brought in his Kingdom. They fought in the ancient tradition of the "Holy War," as men who fight the battle of the Lord, inspired by the possibility that any battle might be the last. At the other extreme the Hellenizers, who had profited by co-operation with foreign rulers and foreign culture, were reluctant to fight, and when they took up arms they did so for political power and advancement. In the beginning the leadership of the revolt was closely allied with the devout party. When religious liberty was won early in the career of Judas the Hammerer, he and his brothers fought on for political independence. More and more they made use of the weapons of diplomacy and foreign alliances, and placed less and less dependence on the direct inspiration and power of God. They were thus forced to come to terms with the pagan culture that they had set out to oppose. The devout progressively drew away from such "apostate" leadership, but they did not draw away as a unity. A wide variety of sects grew up — legalistic, quietistic, moralistic, or monastic, according to the emphasis that seemed most important to each. Meanwhile, the descendants of Mattathias became almost indistinguishable from any other line of petty Eastern monarchs. Judas was commander of the army, supported by the mass of the people; Jonathan was high priest; Simon, high priest *and* ethnarch; Alexander Jannaeus, king. The transformation is complete when we see Jannaeus being pelted with citrons by an angry populace while he was carrying out the functions of high priest.

The Book of Daniel

The strange visions and bizarre language of The Book of Daniel take on new life and meaning when they are seen in the setting in which they were originally intended to be read. The book began to circulate among devout Jews in the early days of the Maccabean Revolt. The result of the uprising was still in doubt; Antiochus was still alive, and the persecutions were going on in full force. To a dispirited and discouraged people the book had one message: Hold on, for the end is near!

The first six chapters of Daniel tell the adventures and perils of four young Jews — Daniel, Shadrach, Meshach, and Abednego — as they try to remain loyal to their faith in a world where steadfastness could mean death. They are required to eat unclean food (ch. 1), to worship an idol (ch. 3), and to offer prayer to the king (ch. 6). The penalties for refusal are the fiery furnace and the den of lions. Yet the young men refuse to obey, and their God delivers them from every peril. The first readers of Daniel knew the temptations, the fires, and the lions from firsthand experience. The book invited them to experience also the deliverance of God.

The theological viewpoint that underlies this section of Daniel is given in chs. 2 and 4. Pagan rulers claim to control the course of history. They say with Nebuchadnezzar, "Is not this great Babylon, which *I* have built by *my* mighty power as a royal residence and for the glory of *my* majesty?" But the real ruler of men and nations is the Most High God, "And his kingdom endures from generation to generation" (ch. 4:34). He weighs, numbers, and judges human kingdoms, and when they prove godless and proud like Belshazzar (ch. 5) he destroys them. The God whose power over history is complete is both able and willing to deliver his faithful servants from the most extreme perils. In the persecutions under Antiochus the words of Daniel (ch. 3:17) must have rung like a battle cry. "Our God whom we serve is able to deliver us . . . and he will deliver us out of your hand, O king."

The theory of history to which the writer of Daniel adhered is spelled out in the visionary sections of the book (chs. 2; 7 to 12). The course of human events has seen four great eras, each more degenerate and godless than the one before: the ages of Babylonia, Media, Persia, and the kingdoms of the Greeks. The four metals of the image (ch. 2) and the four beasts rising from the sea (ch. 7) represent these epochs. Alexander's attack on Persia is described as a battle between a huge goat and a giant ram (ch. 8). The appearance of Antiochus Epiphanes, called " the little horn," is the final triumph of godlessness. He is boastful, vainglorious, proud, a veritable antigod who directs his cruelty against the covenant people. In his time the true God will act and will break his kingdom in pieces and restore the government to Israel, ushering in an age of peace.

If the reader keeps in mind this simple historical clue as he reads the visions of Daniel, much that was obscure will become clear, although the aid of commentaries will be necessary in such complex passages as ch. 11, where the life and times of Antiochus Epiphanes are described in detail.

The Coming of the Romans

The city by the Tiber had a long arm. In 63 B.C. that arm reached to Palestine with Pompey and his legions as its fist. Pompey brought the decaying Seleucid state to an end, and subdued all western Asia for Rome. In Palestine he found two sons of Alexander Jannaeus struggling for their father's throne. The Roman general quickly settled the matter. He stripped Judea of her conquests and placed her under the local control of the high priest with final authority in the hands of the governor of Syria.

Pompey's leadership of the Roman world was by no means secure. He was challenged by Julius Caesar and went down to ruin and defeat. Caesar died soon afterward under the swords of his former friends, who believed him ambitious to become emperor. Only after a protracted period of civil strife (during which the romantic tragedy of Anthony and Cleopatra was played out in Egypt) was Octavius Augustus able to stabilize the government and to make himself the first emperor of the Romans (27 B.C.). In such troubled times an adroit political adventurer can go far. Herod, no true Jew but an Idumaean from the lands south and east of the Dead Sea, maneuvered so skillfully in the changing political scene, and used his native ruthlessness and his small army to such good effect, that he emerged as king of Judea with the blessing (but under the careful scrutiny) of Rome. Herod was a strong ruler and a tireless builder of impressive public works in the Roman style. He undertook to reconstruct the Temple on a scale far larger than it had ever been before, but this grandiose gesture won him no friends. His cruelty and low morals offended his subjects, and he was an Idumaean, descended from the Edomites, Israel's traditional enemies (see, for example, the Book of Obadiah).

After Herod's death (4 B.C.) the administration of the Holy Land alternated between puppet kings and procurators (provincial governors sent out from Rome with wide powers, but subject to the governor of Syria), while in Jerusalem the high priest had considerable authority in local matters. Herod's will divided the Kingdom among his three sons, but Archaelaus, who got Judea, ruled so badly that he was exiled and the first series of procurators was instituted. Pontius Pilate was one of them. About A.D. 40 an easygoing, high-living grandson of Herod was granted the kingship of all his grandfather's territories by the Roman emperor Caligula, and ruled as Herod Agrippa I. His son, Herod Agrippa II, ruled so badly that the procurators (who were not much better) were returned, and continued in authority until revolt broke out in A.D. 66.

This succession of events covers New Testament times. Herod was on the throne when Jesus was born. Pilate, the fifth of the first group of procurators, was in control at the time of the crucifixion, but one of Herod's sons, Herod Antipas, " that fox " (Luke 13:32), still ruled in Galilee, and Luke records that Jesus was tried before him because he was a Galilean. Paul had to defend himself before two members of the second series of procurators, Felix and Festus, and before Herod Agrippa II, who retained some authority under the procurators (Acts, chs. 24 to 26).

The Death of a Nation

From the time of Herod, the Holy Land was continuously teetering on the edge of revolt. Armed bands of zealous patriots roamed the countryside as brigands. The ordinary citizen groaned under oppression, and often kept a sword under his cloak (Luke 22:38) or in his house against the day when the Lord would call him to strike a blow for freedom. In A.D. 66 the procurator Florus marched on the Temple to collect seventeen talents from the treasury. He was met by an armed mob and driven off. The revolt that followed lasted for four years and was ended only when the brilliant general Titus captured Jerusalem after a five-month siege.

After A.D. 70, Palestine lived in an uneasy peace. It was the calm before the storm. Jerusalem lay in ruins and the Temple tax was used to support the temple of Jupiter in Rome. When Hadrian forbade circumcision and made ready to build a temple of Jupiter on the site of the Temple of the Lord, Jewish feeling could stand no more. Led by Bar-Cochba, "the Son of the Star," who had been proclaimed Messiah by Rabbi Akiba, the people rose for one last desperate struggle. With the defeat of the revolt in A.D. 135 the covenant nation ceased to exist in the homeland where it had given birth to two world religions, Judaism and Christianity.

CHAPTER 3 | *The Changing Community*

"Woe to you, scribes and Pharisees, hypocrites! . . . How are you to escape being sentenced to hell? " (Matt. 23:29, 33.) Who were the scribes and Pharisees to draw such stinging words from "the meek and lowly" Jesus? These two classes of people are not the only groups named in the New Testament. We meet also the Sadducees, "who say that there is no resurrection" (Matt. 22:23), and the Herodians, who tried "to entrap him [Jesus] in his talk" (Mark 12:13). Other groups were not so hostile to Jesus and his work. There was a Zealot among his disciples (Luke 6:15). His cousin, John the Baptist, organized his followers into a party that survived long after John's head had been placed on a silver platter to please a dancing girl. Paul met some who had been baptized "into John's baptism" in Ephesus, eight hundred miles from the Jordan where John preached (Acts 19:1-7). The disciples of Jesus must have looked to their contemporaries like one more of the numerous parties into which the Judaism of Palestine was divided.

The Judaism that was thus broken up at home was also scattered abroad. Paul was an indomitable traveler. In his lifetime he covered several thousand miles afoot or by donkey or ship, but wherever he went an important institution was there before him. The Jewish community had fingered out into all the urban centers of the Empire. It was to the local synagogues of the cities on his way that Paul went first of all with his gospel. They were his bridgeheads in the pagan world.

It thus appears that Judaism had undergone a twofold breakup. Physically and geographically it was scattered far beyond Palestine to the four corners of the earth. Internally, and especially in the homeland, it had broken into a considerable number of separate groups, each with its own distinctive doctrines.

If you tie a bucket of water to a piece of rope, you can swing it in a wide circle without spilling a drop. But the water pressing on the bottom of the bucket is under steady tension, and, should the bucket spring a leak or two, the water will fly out all around the circle. From her earliest beginnings, Israel was like the water in the bucket. She was held together by her great, formative ideal. She was the people of God, chosen and made a nation by him, given his covenant law, and bound to live in strictest obedience to his word and will. Nevertheless, the centrifugal forces were always present, keeping Israel under tension and working to break up the nation. The story of the early phases of this struggle is told in other volumes of this series: how the Baalism of Canaan, the deep animosities between the North and the South, and the hammer blows of Assyria and Babylon in turn threatened to destroy Israel, both in ideal and in fact. In the Greek and Roman periods, the history of which has just been briefly sketched, the centrifugal forces came as near as they ever did to breaking up the community. It was toward the end of this period, which saw so many diverse movements *within* Judaism, that Christianity gave the covenant community a new and *international* form in the Christian church.

To understand the New Testament it is necessary to know

something of the religious life of Palestine in which the ministry of Jesus has its setting, and something also of that world-wide Judaism (known as the Dispersion or, technically, the Diaspora) which is the backdrop for the missionary activity of the early church. We shall first consider the Dispersion and then turn our attention to the parties that flourished in Palestine in Jesus' time.

The Diaspora

"Every sea and every land is full of thee (i.e., of the Jews), and every one hateth thee because of thy ways." This sentence from The Sibylline Oracles (3:271-272) was probably written during the Maccabean period, but the Dispersion, which it describes so vividly, was no new thing at that time. After the Assyrian conquests of 721 B.C. and again when the Babylonians destroyed Jerusalem in 586 B.C., pathetic lines of political exiles were forced to make the long trek across desert and mountain from Palestine to the lands along the Tigris and Euphrates, where in bitter despair they hung their harps on the willows and refused to sing the Lord's song in a strange land (Ps. 137:2, 4). Others, like the followers of Johanan (Jer., chs. 40 to 42), fled from their conquered land to sell their swords in the service of Egypt. Many of these exiles followed the advice of Jeremiah to "build houses and live in them; plant gardens and eat their produce" (Jer. 29:5), and neither they nor their descendants were willing to leave the luxuries of the big cities for the frontier life of Palestine when the opportunity arose.

The security and religious tolerance of the Persian Empire gave these exiles a chance to consolidate their position in the pagan world, and the little communities of Jews increased in numbers and influence. The new world, created by the conquests of Alexander and centered in the cities, was ideally suited to a landless people who lived largely by trade and handicrafts. The Dispersion found its way into every considerable city of the Hellenistic world. It bridged the continents and appeared in Europe as well as Asia and North Africa. Among its members were distinguished public officials, soldiers, weavers, goldsmiths, tentmakers, actors, singers, poets, philosophers, sorcerers, and an embarrassingly large number of beggars. By New Testament times a Jewish merchant could take his caravan along excellent Roman roads from the Tigris across Asia Minor and down to Egypt or over to Rome, and be assured at every stopping place of the hospitality of his own people.

A cultured pagan, looking at the Jews in his city, would easily have agreed with the second half of the quotation from The Sibylline Oracles, " Every one hateth thee because of thy ways." The Jews were deliberately and offensively different. They usually lived in their own quarter of the city, grouped around their " house of prayer." They kept away from theaters and public amusements, for which they took little trouble to conceal their contempt. They had peculiar rules of diet that prevented them from sitting at table with non-Jews and from buying food in the public markets. Unlike other races they took no part in the state religion, and regarded those who did as idolaters and little better than atheists. They kept their shops closed on the last day of the week, and practiced a repulsive rite called " circumcision." Besides all this, they were a rowdy lot, always squabbling about theological matters and keeping the city in turmoil (see Acts 18:12-17). They were suspected of robbing pagan temples, and of regarding it as a pious act.

Perhaps our imaginary pagan could have forgiven the Jew for his oddities if he had not been so aggressively superior about them, saying his prayers and doing his ceremonial washings in public places, and forever trying to convert good pagans (Matt. 23:15). Some Jews, it was rumored, thought that their race had a divine mission to be the light of the world and to win the whole of mankind to their faith. These Jewish communities, in return for their support, first of Julius Caesar and then of Augustus, had received special privileges not given to other religious minorities. They were allowed their own council of elders, who governed them in local matters, and they enjoyed religious freedom and exemption from some forms of taxation and state service. Furthermore, their devotion to their families had the disagreeable side effect of increasing their numbers alarmingly, and of making them a more and more formidable element in the population.

Not all pagans were repelled by the Jews and their ways. Every synagogue had its converts and its adherents who were willing to study the doctrine and to obey the moral code, but unwilling to take the final step of circumcision. These "God-fearers," as they were called, were especially receptive to Christianity when it was preached among them (Acts 10:1-2).

What made Judaism attractive to so many pagans? In a world that had too many gods for thoughtful men to believe, Judaism stood for the one God, the creator of all mankind. In a world made skeptical and cynical by too many plausible creeds and philosophies, the Jews claimed to have a divinely given law that could direct all of life in accordance with eternal truth. In a world where vice was commonplace and religion had little to do with morality, the Jew lived by a moral code, strict yet practical. In a world where home life was debased by prostitution and concubinage, Judaism held to the sanctity and purity of the family.

These were powerful recommendations for the Jewish faith, but the real secret of its attractive power lay in the spiritual poverty of the Roman world. The old, heroic ideal of Greece was dead, and in its place a pessimistic fatalism had settled on the minds of men. The gods were discredited, and human virtue was suspect. Men felt themselves slaves to their own passions or to the dark demonic forces of the universe. Neither philosophy nor sensuality, raw superstition nor the many cults of the East (called "mystery religions"), which promised salvation by initiation into their secret knowledge, seemed able to satisfy the persistent question of the age, What shall we do to be saved? The Jewish doctrine of a God who had revealed himself by delivering his people from slavery, and whose very nature was to save, could not but be attractive to many in such a world. Christianity spoke to the same need when it declared, "If the Son makes you free, you will be free indeed" (John 8:36).

Palestinian Judaism

We may now leave the world-wide Judaism of the Dispersion and return to Palestine to see how the meeting of Hellenism and the Jewish faith produced the religious conditions that are familiar to readers of the Gospels.

The Conformists. A conqueror needs some method of administering local affairs in the territories that his armies bring under his rule. In Palestine the Greeks found an instrument ready-made for this purpose. The Israelite monarchy was gone, but the Temple remained as the rallying point of the people. It possessed the four necessities of government: a treasury, a legal code, an organized body of experienced officials, and the respect of the citizens. Since in those days the principle of the separation of church and state did not exist, it was inevitable that the high priest should become head of the local government, and that his staff of priests should acquire both prestige and power.

Power always exacts its price. The ruling priests had no desire to appear unsophisticated or provincial in dealing with those foreign officials on whose good will their position of influence depended. The priestly class thus became the leaders of those who for business or other reasons conformed to the customs of the Greeks. Up to the time of the Maccabean Revolt the high priests ruled, often to the disgust and anger of the common people. The revolt itself was, of course, a low point in the fortunes of the priestly party. Patriotic fervor ran at flood tide. Zeal for the law and love for everything traditionally Jewish swept away, or at least temporarily submerged, the conformist spirit. But as the religious vigor died out of the revolt, and the Maccabean state became a petty kingdom among the kingdoms of the world, the conformists were restored to office and government.

By this time they had formed a definite party, known as the Sadducees, who became supporters and advisors of the Hasmonaean princes. With certain natural ups and downs they retained their position of influence throughout the Roman period. Just before New Testament times a new party appeared in the ranks of the conformists. They were the supporters of the Idumaean adventurer Herod and his family. The Herodians had no religious foundation and existed on the basis of political expediency — the age-old motive of gaining advantages by falling in with the party in power. The Herodians and the Sadducees were both political parties. They lived by politics, and they died when the Roman legions brought an end to political activity in Palestine in A.D. 70.

The Sadducees were conformists, suave, sophisticated, self-assured, and aristocratic, as they appear in the New Testament; but they were not apostates from Judaism. Sympathetically inclined toward Hellenism and desiring to absorb as much as possible from it, the Sadducees wished at the same time to preserve their identity as Jews. This means that they had to define what was absolutely essential to their religion in such a way as to leave themselves the maximum area of freedom to do business with the Hellenistic world. The indispensable minimum of Judaism that the Sadducees recognized was the law, the first five books of the Old Testament. These they regarded as authoritative and binding upon them, and they rejected the authority of the remainder of the Old Testament and the mass of interpretation that had grown up around it.

For example, the Sadducee did not believe in the resurrection because it was not clearly taught in the Mosaic Law, and because it was a relatively new doctrine. His political ambitions made him suspicious of popular belief in the Messiah who would come from God to destroy the Gentile powers.

The Sadducee, moreover, was a ritualist. He tended to believe that as long as the altars smoked in the Temple, and its rituals were faithfully carried out, the demands of religion were being fulfilled. It is easy to think of this as a shallow faith until one remembers that in A.D. 70 the priests continued to officiate at the altar while the Romans were storming the walls, and allowed themselves to be cut down in their places rather than interrupt the sacred rite.

The Sadducean movement was led by priests, but it would be wrong to think of every priest as a conformist. Many of them were as firmly set against admitting foreign elements into their way of life as the staunchest Pharisees. One such was the father of John the Baptist (Luke, ch. 1). The pious, almost monastic sect that produced the Dead Sea scrolls counted not a few priests among their number.

The Resistance. Judaism's powerful resistance to Hellenism was initially the stubborn loyalty of simple men to the ways of their fathers. They clung with great tenacity to the observance of the Sabbath, the practice of circumcision, and the laws of clean and unclean food, not because these things were particularly excellent in themselves, but because they were the signs of the covenant that existed between God and Israel, by virtue of which Israel had her special standing among the nations. Under Ptolemaic rule, the faithful must have suffered much abuse and contempt from the conformists, and Ps. 73 is the pathetic outcry of a man struggling to retain his faith in a world where faith is out of fashion.

With the persecutions under Antiochus Epiphanes the faithful had to endure more than contempt. The death penalty had been decreed for adherence to the traditional practices of their religion. As I Maccabees tells us, "They chose to die, rather than to profane the holy covenant; and they did die." (Ch. 1:63.) Under such desperate stresses the more fanatical left wing of the resistance organized itself into a party called the Hasidim, "the Loyal Ones." When Mattathias raised the standards of revolt in the Judean mountains, the Hasidim buckled on their swords and went out to fight the battle of the Lord, as the heroes of Israel had fought before them.

The Maccabean state that emerged from the revolt was little to the liking of the Hasidim, and, withdrawing their support from it, they returned to the fundamental task of protecting their religion from the perils that surrounded it. They no longer had the strong cement of persecution and battle to hold them together, and the Hasidic party disappeared to be replaced by a variety of parties that were its intellectual children. How many of these once existed we do not now know. But the historian Josephus has preserved the record of three of them: the Zealots, the Essenes, and the Pharisees.

In the Zealots the battle tradition of the Hasidim lived on. The Zealot drew his strength from one of the most ancient elements in the Old Testament tradition: the Holy War. His heroes were the warriors of the Lord — Joshua, David, and Hezekiah. His working faith was that the covenant people would not be allowed to suffer forever under a Gentile yoke.

One day the Messiah of the line of David would appear. The great ram's horn would sound the call to arms, and the armies of Israel would march for the final conflict against the massed might of the pagan world. The people of God would fight, but the victory would be the Lord's. In the time of waiting the Zealots made arrowheads and kept their swords bright. They lost no opportunity to do acts of violence against the Romans, for who could tell what bold stroke would be the trigger that would set off the war of liberation? Many of their number became outlaws, and roamed the country in armed bands. If anyone claimed messiahship, he could count on a following of Zealots. In Jesus' boyhood six thousand of them were hanged for insurrection in Galilee, but in A.D. 70 they were in the forefront of the first revolt. Although they were broken and scattered by the disciplined legions, enough of them remained to spearhead Bar-Cochba's Revolt in A.D. 132. The defeat of that cause was the end of the Zealot movement in Palestine.

The Essenes shared the militant faith of the Zealots, but in a quieter and more reflective way. The question that obsessed them was, Why does not God deliver his people at once? They answered, "Israel, because of her impurity, is unworthy of deliverance." Accordingly, they withdrew from the common life of the villages and towns and formed separate communities in which, uncontaminated by the world, they could practice purity and obedience to the law. Thus, they would be ready when the day of the Lord struck, and the Messiah came. Around the faithful nucleus of their communities the tribes of Israel would be gathered and purified for life in the Messianic Kingdom.

The Essenes retained the rigid piety of the Hasidic movement, and reinforced it by firm organization and strict ritual. A new member was carefully selected and tested by a long period of probation. When he was admitted to the community, he pledged himself to renunciation of all possessions and to complete obedience to his superiors in the order. He wore the white garment of the Essenes and took part in the sacred washings and the ceremonial meals. His days passed away in work, prayer, and the patient study of the Scripture. We shall have a close-up of one such group when in the next chapter we turn our attention to the community by the Dead Sea.

The total breakup of Palestinian Judaism after the two revolts against Rome ended the Essene movement, but did not end its influence. The early Christian church had somewhat similar groups called the Ebionites, "the poor," and in Egypt, contemporaneously with the Essenes, a Jewish society called the Therapeutae lived in small huts, subsisting on vegetables and dedicated to prayer, silence, and the study of the Scripture. The ideals of self-denial and piety that such groups represented never died away in either Judaism or Christianity.

By far the most important of the spiritual descendants of the Hasidim were the Pharisees. They represent a kind of middle way between Zealot and Essene. First and foremost they were men of the law, believing that the salvation of Israel depended on complete devotion to the written Word of God down to its smallest detail. They did not withdraw from society like the Essenes, but worked manfully within the structure of the national life to reform and purify it. They taught in the synagogues, were active in politics, and vigorously missionary toward the Gentiles, making their influence felt in every department of life.

From their first appearance shortly after the Maccabean revolt the Pharisees were immensely popular with the common people. (The story of the crucifixion of Jesus shows how they could raise and sway a mob.) Their profound knowledge of the law and their personal devotion to it, their steady opposition to Hellenistic culture, and their stand against the corrupt

Hasmonaean princes won them the respect of the citizens. This was increased by their deep interest in the education of the people to the demands of the law, and their defense of popular doctrines such as the resurrection and the coming of the Messiah. The determined efforts of the Pharisees to make the law govern the whole of life led them to develop a large body of oral interpretation of the law, designed to answer such questions as "When does the Sabbath begin?" or "What is work?" This oral tradition grew to vast proportions, but to the Pharisee it was all as sacred as the law itself. In Rabbi Akiba's phrase, the oral tradition "built a fence around the law."

The early history of the Pharisees is a stormy tale of struggle against the Sadducees and the Hasmonaean princes. The Pharisees broke with John Hyrcanus amid a flurry of mutual insults and endured vigorous persecution under the cruel hand of Alexander Jannaeus. In the end their firmness and popular esteem won the day. Jannaeus' successor, Queen Alexandra Salome, invited them to be her advisors in government, and they won the seats on the Sanhedrin (the governing council of elders in Jerusalem) that they held in New Testament times. At first the Pharisaic leadership favored Roman intervention in Palestinian affairs. When Rome turned tyrant the Pharisees supported the revolt of A.D. 70. Again in 135 it was a Pharisee, Rabbi Akiba, who declared Bar-Cochba to be Messiah, and thus set in motion the second revolt, although this time there was much misgiving among the Pharisees. After the tragic defeat of Bar-Cochba, the Pharisees set aside the hope of the immediate coming of the Messiah and concentrated on the task of interpreting the law. They thus became the fathers of modern Judaism.

Why is the New Testament, especially the Gospels, so openly anti-Pharisee? The New Testament portrait of the Pharisees, drawn in the heat of controversy, is partial and misleading. It does less than justice to the integrity and earnestness of many members of the group. But the acid quality of the New Testament attacks on Pharisaism indicates that a fundamental issue was at stake between them and the early Christians. Jesus attacked this powerful party principally because of its shallow understanding of righteousness. Obedience to law can readily become mechanical, an external conformity that leaves lust, greed, and self-centeredness untouched. Jesus demanded a righteousness that went beyond that of the Scribes and Pharisees, and that sprang from an inner life attuned to the will of God (Matt. 5:17-20). Jesus also charged the Pharisees with hypocrisy in that they treated with contempt those who were not as rigid in obeying the externals of the law as themselves. Paul continued the fight against the righteousness that comes by the law, contending instead that real righteousness is the gift of God on the basis of faith.

Why did the Pharisees lead the opposition to Jesus? Their popularity and acknowledged leadership seems to have gone to their heads. They regarded as dangerous any popular religious leader who was not one of their number. In the case of Jesus the opposition stiffened because he refused to recognize that the oral tradition so dear to the heart of the Pharisee was equal in authority to the law and, moreover, he claimed a good deal of freedom in interpreting the law itself. His claim to be a direct spokesman for God in the manner of the Old Testament prophets, and the suspicion that he might be making Messianic claims for himself, both contributed to the Pharisees' hostility to Jesus.

The Disinherited

History deals with generals, statesmen, and political parties. The man who tends his nets or sells his vegetables is generally forgotten. The ordinary citizen of Palestine was an impoverished peasant in an overpopulated land. Looked down on by the aristocratic Sadducee, held in contempt by some of the Pharisees because he could not know or obey the whole law, betrayed by the native princes, and exploited for taxes by foreign overlords, he was one of the *am ha-aretz,* " the people of the land," the disinherited of Israel. But he had two things that could not be taken from him — his memory and his hope. From Sinai his family had been part of the people of the Lord. The loving care of God and the promises of God belonged to him as much as to the great of the land. He knew his God as one who " has put down the mighty from their thrones, and exalted those of low degree "; who " has filled the hungry with good things, and the rich he has sent empty away " (Luke 1:52-53). His hope was that God would again put down the mighty, and the day would dawn when " they shall sit every man under his vine and under his fig tree, and none shall make them afraid " (Micah 4:4). The faith of the disinherited is admirably summarized by Luke in his description of Simeon: they were " righteous and devout, looking for the consolation of Israel " (ch. 2:25).

The situation of the oppressed peasant in Israel explains the tremendous power of messianic ideas in the period between the Testaments. It shows also why the common people heard Jesus' message gladly, and why in the early church " not many were powerful " (I Cor. 1:26).

Chapter 4 | *The Dead Sea Sect*

The Romans worshiped a god, Janus, the deity of doorways and beginnings, who had two faces and could look in both directions at once. This is a kind of Janus chapter. We have surveyed the literature, the world events, and the internal condition of Judaism in the inter-Testamental period. Before beginning an examination of the religious thought of the period, we shall pause in this chapter to follow the fortunes of the amazing Jewish sect that flourished beside the Dead Sea from sixty-five years before Christ to seventy years after. Its history will give us a backward look over events with which we are now familiar, and its manuscripts will introduce us to the religious concerns of the age. We shall have the additional advantage of dealing with a single small group that has left a wealth of information about itself in the fascinating documents known as the Dead Sea scrolls.

The Community at Qumrân

The view eastward from Jerusalem is all Palestine in miniature. In the immediate foreground, the rolling uplands of Judea stretch away to the east. Cultivated valleys lie among gray ridges, and terraced farms run like stairways up the mountainside. Here and there a cluster of flat-roofed houses and a tall minaret mark the presence of a little village where the farmers live. Farther east the highlands merge into a sterile, jagged, red-gray wasteland where the sheep of the tent-dwelling Bedouin roam restlessly in search of the few patches of green among the rocks. This is the wilderness where John the Baptist lived, and from which he came out to preach. Beyond this, a vivid, sky-blue mirror, is the fascinating lake that we call the Dead Sea and the Hebrew people named the Sea of Salt. On its eastern shore the rugged face of the mountains of Moab rise like a red wall. A small rounded knob is Mt. Nebo, from which the dying Moses saw the Promised Land.

Anyone who left the relative prosperity of the highlands to live in the wilderness must have had a compelling reason. Down there, several hundred feet below sea level, the heat is blistering, food hard to get, and water almost nonexistent. The only rewards the region can give its inhabitants are solitude, silence, and some of the most breath-taking scenery on earth. But the impulses of religion were strong enough to make the Dead Sea community leave the security of established villages and build a home for itself on the edge of the wilderness.

A dry watercourse — the Arabs call it a "wadi" — is no rarity in Palestine. The face of the country is scarred with them everywhere. The Wâdī Qumrân begins a few miles east of Jerusalem and breaks out of the Judean Highlands near the northeast corner of the Dead Sea. Where it emerges on the mile-wide flats by the sea there is a plateau, some four hundred feet high, and close by on the seashore is a beautiful little spring. On this plateau, with the mountains at their back and the spring at their feet, the Dead Sea community erected its buildings. They were begun about 150 B.C., when John Hyrcanus was ruling in Jerusalem and the Sadducean party was riding high in power. They were used in one way or another until A.D. 135. After this they lay in ruins until an archaeological expedition under the direction of Father Roland de Vaux brought their story to light in the nineteen fifties.

The main building was a rectangular, two-story structure, roughly one hundred by two hundred feet. One corner was reinforced to form a guard tower with storerooms below and three long narrow rooms above. There were a number of such narrow rooms with benches around the walls in the building. For the most part they seemed to be meeting rooms, but one of them had been fitted out with writing tables, complete with inkwells and washbasins for the scribes. The building was equipped with a dining hall and pantry (about a thousand dishes were found there), an elaborate privy, a pottery-making center, and a large oven. The whole layout suggested that the building was the headquarters of a much larger group than could live within its walls.

This group had a passion for water equal to its interest in writing and in places of meeting. They dammed up one branch of the Wâdī Qumrân to catch the flow that came down in the rainy season, and conveyed the water in a stone channel to the building where it was stored in a complex system of cisterns. Perhaps all this water was for domestic purposes, but the large quantities stored in the building in addition to the spring nearby suggests that the water was used in religious rituals.

The dead of the community were buried on the plateau just outside the building in a cemetery that contained about a thousand graves. A three- or four-foot shaft was dug, and a burial chamber excavated to one side. Here the body was laid, head to the south, hands folded on the hips, with no funeral offerings or possessions of any kind beside it. The entrance to the chamber was blocked off, the shaft filled in, and an oval of stones left to mark the place. A strict religious sect might well be responsible for such simple funeral practices.

The run-of-the-mill member of the group did not live in the

buildings themselves. His home was most likely a tent or other flimsy structure along the cliffs near the monastery. The caves of the region provided ready-made storehouses for household articles and worn-out or unused manuscripts. When danger threatened, the most valuable documents were wrapped in linen, placed in tall jars, and put away for safety in the caves. This was a wise precaution, for in A.D. 68, during the first revolt, the building was burned to the ground and its occupants dispersed. They did not come back. The Romans rebuilt the structure as a guardhouse and garrisoned it with troops of the Tenth Legion. Bar-Cochba's forces occupied it briefly during the second revolt, and afterward it stood a silent ruin in the wilderness, the caves around preserving in their dry interiors the manuscripts that set the scholarly world buzzing in 1947.

These manuscripts are the key to the mystery of the buildings. Without them we should have only snippets of information about the Dead Sea community. Indeed, if the Dead Sea scrolls had not been discovered, the buildings would probably never have been excavated. Even after the scroll finds, an uncomfortably large number of question marks and "perhapses" remain. Nevertheless, the manuscripts give us surprisingly intimate glimpses of the life and thought of the community by the sea. The important point about the ideas revealed in the scrolls is that they were not the exclusive property of this one sect. The probability is that Jesus spoke to men and women who held convictions much like those of the sect. The Dead Sea scrolls provide a new and wider window into the Judaism that existed between the Testaments.

A Teacher of Righteousness Arises

"And as for what it says, that he may run who reads it, this means the teacher of righteousness, to

> whom God made known all the mysteries of the words of his servants the prophets." (The Habakkuk Commentary.)
>
> "The wicked priest . . . persecuted the teacher of righteousness in order to confound him in the indignation of his wrath." (The Habakkuk Commentary.)

The roots of the Dead Sea community must reach back to the aftermath of the Maccabean Revolt, when the hopes of the religious were being shattered by the worldliness of the Hasmonaean princes. The Damascus Document probably refers to this time when it says, "They were like men blind and groping for the way for twenty years." Some, at least, of the searchers found a faith to believe and a man to follow. "God observed their works, that they sought him with a perfect heart; and he raised up for them a teacher of righteousness to lead them in the way of his heart." (The Damascus Document.)

Who was this Teacher and what did he accomplish? He is altogether a shadowy and mysterious figure, but out of scattered references to him in the commentaries of the sect and from one of the thanksgiving hymns, which rings like personal experience and may be a poetic autobiography of the Teacher, we can form some idea of his life and work.

He was probably a member of a high-ranking priestly family, born into the party that was leading the people away from the ancient ways toward the culture and customs of the Greeks. He realized that the community of the people of God was being broken up, and that the covenant on which the destiny of Israel depended was being undermined and destroyed. He felt himself involved in this apostasy, guilty because of it, and separated from God. Like Isaiah before him, he was rescued from despair by a sense of forgiveness, and a conviction that God had chosen him to do certain work. The "autobiographical" hymn describes this experience.

> "For I remember my guilty deeds,
> together with the faithlessness of my fathers. . . .
> Then I said, 'For my transgression
> I am left outside of thy covenant.'
> But when I remembered the strength of thy hand,
> together with the abundance of thy mercy,
> I rose and stood up, and my spirit became strong."

He became a preacher in defense of the law. With a prophetic accent, he accused his contemporaries of idolatry and of "serving God with a double heart." He condemned their leaders as "false prophets, enticed by error," "planning the devices of Belial," and "speaking with a foreign tongue" (Greek?). This preaching would not go down well with the Sadducean authorities. The Wicked Priest and the Man of the Lie, to give them the picturesque names used in The Habakkuk Commentary, ruthlessly opposed the Teacher, and may have driven him into exile.

However, the courage of the man and the power of his message attracted followers. He was a student of the Scriptures, and from his study he developed a set of regulations, the heart of the law and "the way of perfection." He not only taught his followers this "way," but apparently organized them into a community that was to be the true Israel, the real sons of the covenant. They called themselves "the sons of light."

We can only guess that mounting persecution, which may have claimed the Teacher's life, forced his disciples to withdraw to the plateau by the Wâdī Qumrân. After the death of the Teacher the community continued to live by the Dead Sea, studying the Scriptures, obeying the rule, and waiting for the

Day of the Lord, and the long-delayed victory of their cause.

The striking parallels between the Teacher of Righteousness and Jesus of Nazareth have attracted widespread attention. His knowledge of the Scriptures, his sense of mission, his willingness to endure persecution, the reverence in which he was held by his followers, and the community that he founded are impressive points of similarity. The appearance of a teacher of this kind in the inter-Testamental period, the attractive power of his message, and the treatment he received show clearly that the prophetic line did not die out between the Testaments. Its witness was kept continuously alive by men like the Teacher. Although we do not know his name, the Teacher of Righteousness stands like a living bridge between the prophets and Christ.

The Law for a New Israel

> "All who come into the order of the community shall pass over into the covenant before God, to do according to all that he has commanded, and not to turn away from following him because of any dread or terror or trial or fright in the dominion of Belial. And when they pass into the covenant, the priests and the Levites shall bless the God of salvation and all his works of truth; and all those who are passing into the covenant shall say after them, 'Amen! Amen!'" (The Manual of Discipline.)

The Teacher and his community would have agreed with Paul's words to the Ephesians: "We are not contending against flesh and blood, but against the principalities, against the powers, against *the world rulers of this present darkness,* against *the spiritual hosts of wickedness in the heavenly places*" (ch. 6:12). The whole universe is involved in a life-and-death struggle between light and darkness. In the heavenly places the angels of God stand against the powers of evil under their prince, Belial. In human history the Gentile nations oppose the people of God. Within every human being the elements of light and darkness, truth and perversity, are mingled, and struggle for the mastery of the soul. To a degree the proportion of light to darkness in a person's character is fixed, and can be measured by the position of the stars at his birth. The Dead Sea community, therefore, believed in and practiced astrology. But they were not complete fatalists. By determined self-discipline a man could beat the darkness out of his nature and help make himself a "son of light." The New Testament, and John's Gospel in particular, frequently uses the idea of a cosmic struggle between light and darkness.

The world history, which we have been reviewing in the last two chapters, seemed to the community like a depressing record of victory piled on victory for the forces of darkness. They had seized control of the whole Gentile world. Using the Greek and Roman armies as their instruments, they had overrun the Holy Land. They had corrupted its political life, debased the sacred priesthood, and led many in Israel into idolatry. Their vicious godlessness had been at its worst in the persecution of the Teacher of Righteousness. Such deep darkness must mean that dawn was near and "the dominion of Belial" almost over.

The community had not gone into the wilderness to enjoy solitude for its own sake, but to save Israel by establishing the New Covenant that Jeremiah had foretold (ch. 31:31-34). In the last days of human history they would make a society from which every trace of darkness was excluded. When God acted to annihilate the powers of evil, he could use this pure community as the spearhead of his attack, and the center around which to gather a New Israel.

The purity of the community was most in danger when a new member joined its ranks. The recruit could easily bring evil influences with him from outside and let darkness in among the sons of light. The Manual of Discipline describes how the community kept out the wicked, the weak, and the doubtful. A candidate for admission remained on probation for at least three years. He studied the law of Moses and the doctrines of the sect, and four times he came before the solemn assembly for a searching examination of his knowledge and character. Those who survived this intensive screening were enrolled among " the Many," as the full members of the sect were called.

The Many had no private possessions, everything was " mingled " in a common fund. To us this may seem a doubtful blessing, but to the Dead Sea sect it was the visible sign that they were a true community, sharing all resources both spiritual and physical. This strong sense of " togetherness " is characteristic of Old Testament Israel, and the early church was " communistic " for a time for much the same reason as the sect (Acts 2:43-47).

Since discipline and self-denial were necessary to keep the community faithful to its covenant and free from darkness, the life of the sectarian was deliberately made difficult. He was part of an iron-clad legal system, administered by officers with forbidding titles — Overseer, Inspector, and Judge. At all banquets and general meetings he had to take his place according to his assigned rank, and he could speak in the assembly only if given permission to do so. Spitting during a meeting could cost him three months' punishment; ill-considered laughter, thirty days; grumbling against " the institution of the community," banishment for life. One third of the time he had to stay up all night, studying with the brothers and singing hymns. In all matters the priests had authority over the laymen, and no meeting of more than ten persons could be held unless a priest were present. The Levites acted as a police force to see that the innumerable rules were obeyed and to keep every man in his place. If sects like this were widely known in Jesus' day, one can see why questions of rank and precedence appear so often in the New Testament (for example, Luke 14:7-11; Matt. 20:20-28).

Two of the community's rituals remind one of the Christian sacraments of Baptism and the Lord's Supper. Sacred baths were celebrated at Qumrân, but where, or how, or even why is not at all certain, since references to the ceremony are scattered and obscure. For example, The Damascus Document tells us little except that the water must be clean, and sufficient to cover the body. The sect may have used the rite, as the early Christians did, in the initiation of new members, but probably sacred baths were taken periodically by all members as a symbol of purity. At Qumrân every meal had religious significance, but from time to time the Many gathered for a formal ritual banquet. This feast was a dramatic rehearsal for the messianic banquet that would take place when the victory over Belial's forces was won and God's Kingdom established.

A third ritual of the community, the annual renewing of the covenant, has Old Testament overtones (see Josh., ch. 24; Deut., ch. 27; Neh., chs. 8 to 10). If the reader will imagine the white-robed brothers drawn up in ranks on the rocky plateau in the wilderness with the dead land around and the Dead Sea in front, dedicating themselves to absolute obedience to the covenant in spite of "dread or terror or trial or fright in the dominion of Belial," he will catch something of the spirit of this strange sect. The priests recount God's mighty acts and his promises to his people. The Levites make a grim antiphon, reciting the curses that rest on the men of Belial. A chorus of "amens" answers each recitation. Then the community "passes over" into the covenant (perhaps by baptism); first the priests, then the Levites, and then the people, each in his assigned place.

Interpreting the Scripture

> "The Many shall keep watch together a third of all the nights of the year, reading the book and searching for justice, and worshiping together." (The Manual of Discipline.)

The sectarians followed the example of their Teacher in searching many books. For the community to remain free of darkness, it had to know God's law and the interpretation of the law that the Teacher had made. Mechanical memorizing was not enough. Understanding was required to see the inner meaning of the law. It is typical of the sect that its members studied together in the attitude of worship. No individualism was permitted, even to a bookworm.

The basic documents for legal study were the five books of Moses. In them the terms of the original covenant between God and Israel were recorded, and in them "everything was specified." The sect had other legal books that were studied alongside the law. Important among them was a handbook for beginners, called The Book of Hagi. One example of the sect's legal activity is its interpretation of the Mosaic commandment, "Remember the sabbath day, to keep it holy." The Damascus Document lists twenty-seven laws that define the meaning of Sabbath observance.

The numerous other sacred writings that the sect recognized were treated differently from the law. The books were believed to contain divine "mysteries"—a favorite word of the sect and of Paul. The plain meaning of the text was not its real meaning. Truth was concealed in it that, if brought to light, would reveal the hidden purposes of God. Out of the study of these mysteries the community developed a novel type of Biblical commentary. A portion of the text was quoted, and its hidden meaning was given. This almost invariably referred to the history or special interests of the sect itself. Thus any good man mentioned in the text was identified with the Teacher of Righteousness, and every wicked man became the Wicked Priest. The Qumrân community read its own history and doctrine into every sacred text it studied, a habit still in vogue in some modern Christian groups. Many examples of this kind of commentary have turned up among the Dead Sea literature, and composing them must have been one of the main tasks of " the watchers " of Qumrân.

This method of handling Scripture was no monopoly of the Qumrân community. Both Philo and Paul used allegory to uncover a hidden meaning under the surface of Old Testament stories (compare Paul's treatment of Sarah and Hagar in Gal. 4:21-31). The Pharisees and Jesus interpreted and expanded the law (Matt. 5:17-48). The Gospel writers often read the history of Christianity into Old Testament prophecy, sometimes flying in the face of the obvious meaning of the text. Matthew, for example, does this when he sees the exodus of Israel from Egypt as a prophecy of Jesus' return from that country (Matt. 2:13-15). The Dead Sea scrolls provide a mass of new material for investigating the fascinating question, How were the scriptures interpreted in New Testament times?

The War to End Wars

> " There shall be a great tumult against the sons of Japheth; and Assyria shall fall with none to help him. And the dominion of the Kittim shall come to an end, so that wickedness shall be laid low with-

out any remnant; and there shall be no survivor of the sons of darkness." (The War of the Sons of Light with the Sons of Darkness.)

According to The Habakkuk Commentary, the "last period" of world history had already extended "beyond what all the prophets had said," and the day of God's action was overdue. When that day came, a prophet would appear to announce its arrival. Then God would send out his *two* Messiahs, the one a priest and the other a soldier. The priestly Messiah of the House of Zadok would probably be none other than the Teacher of Righteousness, restored to life and given the authority that his persecutors had denied him in his first existence. The military Messiah, of the line of David and bearing the title "Prince of Israel," would be charged with the task of leading the armies of God in the last battle against the powers of darkness. The traditional leadership of Israel during Old Testament times would thus be restored in the New Israel. The anointed priest and the anointed prince would stand shoulder to shoulder in the government of the people, as Solomon and Zadok had done centuries before; only with our sect the priest was a far more important figure than the prince.

The process of restoration was now carried from the leadership to the nation as a whole. Israel, scattered in the Dispersion, would be gathered together as Ezra had gathered them after the Babylonian exile. They would come to the community, where the light of true knowledge had been kept alive through the period of darkness, and the priests of the community would instruct them in the regulations of the New Covenant. Out of a renewed nation would emerge the true Israel, without uncleanness and perfectly obedient to God.

The covenant would be sealed by a great messianic feast. The leaders of Israel would take their places at the banquet in their proper order: first, the priestly Messiah with his retinue of priests and Levites, then the Prince of Israel with his officers according to their rank, and, lastly, the heads of the families and the wise men. Each would bless the food in turn, beginning with the priest, and they would eat together in token of the new era that had come. This was the meal for which the sacred banquets of the community were rehearsals.

The task of purification was not yet complete. Israel would be restored, but the world would still lie in darkness. Here the cure was to be as radical as the surgeon's knife: a war "of eternal destruction against all the lot of Belial." It is not to be a war in any realistic sense, but rather a gigantic sacrificial ritual. The age of the soldiers will correspond to the ages of the priests in the Old Testament, and the camps are to be kept ceremonially clean because they are holy places. Everything will happen according to a predetermined pattern. The slogans on the banners and trumpets, the number of charges and countercharges, the exact battle order of the troops, the prayers to be said before and after the fighting, and even the number of javelins to be thrown in each engagement are prescribed. It is a war, not of men only, but of angels as well. Michael and the holy angels will fight for Israel, and the hosts of Belial support the enemy. After forty years, the same time as the wilderness wanderings after the exodus, the final victory is to be won. The forces of Edom, Moab, Ammon, Philistia, and the Kittim (the Romans) are to be destroyed. Now, after so much suffering, God will give "light in joy to all Israel, peace and blessing to the lot of God, to exalt among the gods the rule of Michael and the dominion of Israel over all flesh."

This reconstruction of the thought of the sect about the "last days" is pieced together from the Rule of the Congregation and the War scroll, with help from the other documents. The order of events may be wrong in places, but the general picture must be close to the truth. The reader will notice many similarities to the thought of the New Testament, and many others have been omitted for the sake of brevity. To take only one example, was Jesus thinking of the messianic feast at the end of time when he said, "I shall not drink again of the fruit of the vine *until that day when I drink it new in the kingdom of God*" (Mark 14:25)?

The weight of informed opinion today regards the Dead Sea sect as an Essene community, and holds that the scrolls give authentic and illuminating background for the New Testament. But Jesus was not an Essene, and the church not just another Qumrân. The sect believed in justification by faith in the Teacher of Righteousness, and held that purity was a gift of God, convictions akin to those of the New Testament. However, this sect could never have captured the Gentile world, which it hated, and it could never have freed itself from the law.

CHAPTER 5 | *The Present Age*

NEBUCHADNEZZAR, King of Babylon, had a dream, which, as soon as he awoke, he forgot until Daniel recalled it to his mind (Dan., ch. 2). The king had seen a towering statue with a golden head, a silver breast, a bronze torso, and iron legs. The feet on which the giant image stood were a crumbling mixture of iron and clay. In the dream a stone cut from a mountain by a supernatural power came whirling toward the statue, struck against its feet, and brought the huge figure crashing to the ground.

Daniel was given to such visions in Technicolor. Among his most spectacular was the dream of the two-horned ram and the one-horned goat (ch. 8). A giant ram appeared on the eastern horizon and drove toward the west, smashing all before it, until it came face to face with a massive, raging goat. The two beasts rushed together, and the goat gored the ram to the ground and trampled its prostrate body. Then, before the astonished eyes of the dreamer, the goat began to grow and the horn divided itself into four. A tiny horn sprouted and increased in size until in its pride it began to strike the stars from the sky; but in the end the little-horn-grown-large was destroyed by superhuman power.

This dreaming is not just fun. It is the result of a carefully considered view of human history. On the surface the visions are vivid summaries of the well-known historical facts outlined in Chapter 2. Nebuchadnezzar's image represented the succession of kingdoms that followed the fall of Jerusalem: Babylonia (the head), Media (the chest), Persia (the torso), and Alexander's Hellenistic kingdom (the legs). In the age of mixed strength and weakness (the feet), which came with the death of Alexander, God would act to smash the structure of man-made empires and to establish the Kingdom of his own people (the stone cut " by no human hand," ch. 2:36-45). The battling goat and ram portray the struggle between Alexander of Macedonia and the Persian Empire. The four horns are the divisions of the Hellenistic empire after Alexander's death, and the proud " little horn " is Antiochus Epiphanes, archenemy of the Jewish religion. Although his attack on the people of God succeeded in knocking some stars from the sky, he would eventually be broken " by no human hand " (ch. 8:18-26).

Under the surface the visions are a startlingly consistent interpretation of the events that they describe, an interpretation notably different from that which the prophets of an earlier day had offered. This apocalyptic view of human affairs has five noteworthy features:

1. History is divided, like the body of a tapeworm, into a series of segments.
2. Each of these is worse than the one before, so that history is revealed as a record of the progressive deterioration of mankind.
3. The increasing evil directs itself more and more vigorously against the community of God's people.
4. God is absent from the direct control of affairs, and confines himself to occasional deliverances of his people from the fury of their persecutors.
5. Nevertheless, when the time is ripe, God will reassert his

authority and bring to an end the whole sorry mess into which human history has fallen.

The Times Grow Old

The concept of history tumbling down by stages to a fatal end, like a man falling down stairs, is found not only in Daniel. It is thoroughly characteristic of inter-Testamental thought. The Qumrân community reflected it in their conviction that they were living in the "period of wrath," the "era of Belial" at "the end of the days." The book of Tobit has it in rudimentary form when it states that Jerusalem will not be rebuilt in splendor "until the times of the age are completed" (Tobit 14:5). And this concept lies behind the widespread conviction of the period that the inspiring activity of the Holy Spirit ceased at the time of Ezra. Second Esdras outlines the concept with melancholy precision.

> "The age has lost its youth, and the times begin to grow old. For the age is divided into twelve parts, and nine of its parts have already passed, as well as half the tenth part. . . . Evils worse than you have now seen happen shall be done hereafter. For the weaker the world becomes through old age the more shall evils be multiplied among its inhabitants. For truth shall go farther away, and falsehood shall come near." (II Esdras 14:10-12, 16-18.)

This comparison of history to an aging man, growing weaker and more vicious year by year, grates harshly on modern ears. The optimistic ideal of progress, by which American culture is accustomed to test history, is here replaced by a doctrine of inevitable degeneration, expressed in an unattractive static framework of a series of ages succeeding one another with the mathematical regularity and predictability of numbers in a series. Nine and a half times are passed: two and a half remain. (II Esdras 14:11-12.) History has not the smooth unity of a motion picture, but the jerky discontinuity of a set of bad slides.

Nevertheless, this pessimistic view of history is a bridge between the Testaments. Growing directly out of the prophetic teaching, it preserved that teaching in an age when there was every reason to doubt its validity. It led by a straight road into the New Testament, where it became one of the means by which the early church interpreted the work of Jesus Christ.

Hope Deferred

"Hope deferred makes the heart sick." (Prov. 13:12.) It also makes the brain active. The inter-Testamental writers, constructing their systems of world history, were driven to the task by a long and painful delay in the prophetic hope for Israel. The Old Testament prophets had taught that Israel could fulfill her destiny under God only by holding her national life firm and true to the purpose that God had put before her when he entered into covenant with the nation at Sinai. But the record of Israel had been one of rebellion against the will of God and high treason against his sovereignty. For the intention of God, Israel had substituted her own programs, relying on her army and her wits rather than on the power of her God. The prophets interpreted the destruction of Jerusalem by the Babylonians and the exile of her best citizens as a deserved punishment and a necessary purging of Israel. Like a refiner of gold, Yahweh had put his people into the fire, in order to burn away the dross and leave the pure metal (Zech. 13:9). After the exile the pure gold of the nation, having passed through the fire, would be restored to its homeland, there to live under a Davidic king in faithful obedience to God, enjoying an era of peace and prosperity. The prophetic view of history just described may be diagramed (with allowance for oversimplification) as follows:

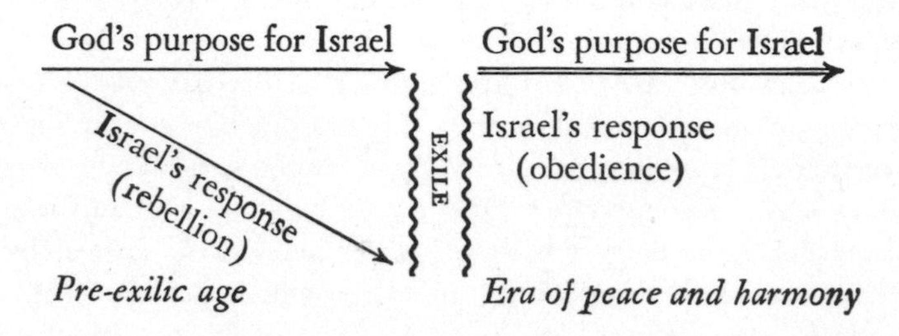

Precisely because the inter-Testamental writers took the prophets seriously, they were thrust into an agonizing problem. The bad had been realized, but the good had not. Punishment had come, as the prophets had foreseen, but peace and prosperity had not followed. Instead, the old rebellious spirit had reasserted itself, and new punishments in the form of persecutions under Antiochus Epiphanes had fallen upon Israel. The brief time of hope during the first high fervor of the Maccabean Revolt had dissolved like morning mist in the power struggles of the Hasmonaean princes. A new diagraming of the historical process was thus forced on the inter-Testamental writers.

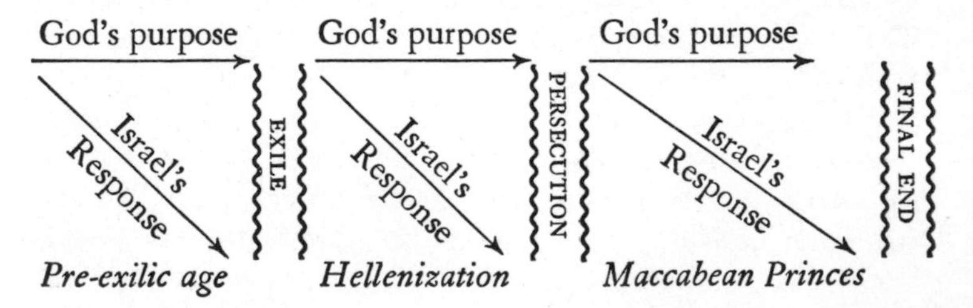

A glance at the second diagram will show why history was blacked off in a series of degenerating ages. The cycle of rebellion-punishment-rebellion seemed to be self-perpetuating, with no means to get off the treadmill except to be lifted from it by the hand of God. Inter-Testamental literature had no quarrel with the prophetic view of God, and of his ultimate control in human affairs. Where the prophets had gone astray was in treating sin too lightly. They had underestimated its deeply entrenched power and the firmness of its grip on human nature, and had expected to be rid of it by a great act of national repentance. The inter-Testamental writers saw that the whole structure of the human enterprise, which we call history, is so interwoven with and involved in the results of man's rebellion against God that when sin goes history goes with it.

Habakkuk, at a much earlier period, had advised his people that " if it [the vision] seem slow, wait for it " (Hab. 2:3). The man of steadfast faith could be content to wait with patient endurance, but, if his intellect was awake, he had to ask himself, " Why does the vision tarry? " For the religious man this took the form of a related question, What is God doing?

What Is God Doing?

When Belshazzar of Babylon gave his great feast for a thousand of his lords, the fingers of a man's hand silently wrote his doom on the plaster of the palace wall (Dan. 5:1-9). Called in to interpret the mysterious writing, Daniel spoke these words to the king: " You have lifted up yourself against the Lord of Heaven; . . . and you have praised the gods of silver and gold, of bronze, iron, wood, and stone, which do not see or hear or know, but the God in whose hand is your breath, and whose are all your ways, you have not honored " (v. 23). In this quotation the principal ingredients of the inter-Testamental view of God appear. He is the one God of all the earth, and the idols, called gods by the pagan nations, are merely inanimate lumps of wood and stone. By contrast with transient earthly monarchies, " his kingdom is an everlasting kingdom " (ch. 4:3), and his universal rule extends even to the breath that men draw. " Good things and bad, life and death, poverty and wealth, come from the Lord." (Ecclus. 11:14.)

Such universal power would be an intolerable dictatorship if it were not exercised in mercy.

> " The compassion of man is for his neighbor,
> but the compassion of the Lord is for all living beings."
> (Ecclus. 18:13.)

The compassion of God does not, however, prevent his punishing sin. In fact his mercy toward the oppressed only makes his anger burn more vigorously toward the oppressor, and his righteousness renders him intolerant of pride and godlessness. The inter-Testamental literature is full of the dark colors of judgment, to which the Dead Sea community gave typical expression in The Habakkuk Commentary: " Their toil [shall be] in vain, to the end that they may come into judgments of fire, because they reviled and insulted God's elect." The tension between the mercy and the judgment of God — latent in the Old Testament — became acute in the inter-Testamental period, and it was usually resolved by confining the divine mercy to the righteous and putting off the complete realization of divine judgment until the end of time.

A tendency to see God as increasingly remote from the world may be seen developing within the Old Testament. The J writer (about 950 B.C.) pictured God walking in the Garden of Eden in face-to-face conversation with human beings (Gen. 3:8-19). In the year that King Uzziah died (742 B.C.), Isaiah could say, " I saw the Lord " (Isa. 6:1), but one hundred and fifty years later Ezekiel was more guarded in his language. He saw "the appearance of the likeness of the glory of God" (Ezek. 1:28) — God four times removed from man. The radical difference between heaven and earth, God and man, was heavily underscored by the inter-Testamental writers. Their names for God — "Ancient of Days," "Lord of Heaven," "Sovereign Lord," "Most High" — are coldly remote and majestic. Second Esdras expresses the spirit of the age when he calls God "he whose dwelling is not with men" (II Esdras 5:38).

As a consequence of this exalted view of God, the inter-Testamental writers focused sharply on the doctrine of Creation. They often retold the story of the seven days that made the universe (for example, II Esdras 3:1-6; 6:38-59; The Book of Jubilees 2:1-33; II Enoch 24:2). Although they were not always of one mind as to whether God worked with formless matter (Wisd. of Sol. 11:17), or whether he created out of nothing (II Enoch 24:2), they were wholly agreed that the ordering of nature was the most profound witness to the character of God. Creation is the one doctrine that best expresses both sovereign control of the universe and "otherness" from man. In creation, as nowhere else, God is being "God, and not man."

Such an emphasis on the oneness, otherness, universality, sovereignty, and creativity of God provides an answer to the question, What is God doing? The answer amounts to a two-sided confession of faith. However much political and economic events seem to deny it, God is in control of his world, of man, and of history, but the details of the divine purpose are beyond human comprehension. The mind staggers and falls helpless before the impossible task of understanding either the infinite wisdom by which God works, or "the goal of love" that he has promised his people. God is doing things, but in his own way, and man can no more " understand the way of the Most High " than he can " make the withered flowers bloom again." And God is acting in his own time. " The creation cannot make more haste than the Creator." What is God doing? He is doing what in his incomprehensible wisdom pleases himself.

The quotations in the last paragraph are from II Esdras 5:21-56, which is well worth reading as an expression of the inter-Testamental doctrine of God.

Enter Evil, with Hosts

A theology that rests on the inscrutable purposes of an all-wise and all-powerful God may satisfy the cloistered saint, but a man who travels the hard road of ridicule and persecution for his faith is more likely to find himself in sympathy with the old folk song: " Don't see it clearly this side of Jordan." If God's in his heaven, why is not all right with the world? The inter-Testamental writers gave a one-word answer: *sin*. Through Moses, God had given his law for the guidance and salvation of the nation, but another force was at work in opposition to the law (II Baruch, chs. 17; 18). It is the " evil heart " of man (II Esdras 3:20-27). Out of a corrupt inner life proceed deeds of violence and oppression. The inner corruption projects itself outward into history, polluting it and making it evil. Because of " the evil heart," man is alienated from God and becomes the victim of suffering and death (II Esdras 7:48). Thus man, not God, creates sin (I Enoch 98:4). God has placed an impulse to evil in man, but he has given him the power to overcome it if he desires to do so (Ecclus. 15:14-20).

Every human being is engaged in a contest with the evil impulse. The prize is life, and the penalty for failure, death (II Esdras 7:47). In rare cases, individuals of a particularly strong moral character may win, but no *nation* has ever overcome evil (ch. 3:36). The melancholy fact of history is that evil overcomes good.

How did the evil impulse in human nature originate? The inter-Testamental literature is very reluctant to place the blame on God, and in one or two passages emphatically denies that God created evil (Ecclus. 15:11-13). But if God created everything that exists, it is not easy to clear him of all responsibility for the existence of sin. The usual inter-Testamental way out of the difficulty was to fall back on Gen., chs. 2 and 3, and to trace the origin of sin and death to the disobedience of Adam and Eve (Ecclus. 25:24; II Baruch 23:4). Second Esdras uses the metaphor of growing grain. Adam possessed a tiny seed of evil, which by his disobedience he allowed to get the better of him. This little seed propagated itself generation by generation until it produced a great harvest of evil (ch. 4:30). Or the figure is sometimes that of a fatal, infectious disease, contracted by Adam and " caught " by his descendants (ch. 3:22).

Although Adam's sin brought death to all, it does not relieve anyone of responsibility for his own sin. " Each of us has been the Adam of his own soul." (II Baruch 54:19.) God gives each individual the choice of light (the law) or darkness (the sin of Adam). A few take their light from the law; many take their darkness from Adam (ch. 18:2).

With the inter-Testamental doctrine of sin in mind, we can understand the struggles of the Qumrân sect and of the early church to produce a community devoted to God's purpose, an enterprise that had never successfully been carried out in human history. And we can understand Paul's monumental wrestling with the doctrine of the First and Second Adam (Rom., ch. 5; I Cor. 15:20-28). It is no great exaggeration to maintain that the inter-Testamental doctrine of sin is the necessary background of the New Testament doctrine of salvation.

Many intelligent people regarded the evil heart of man as

inadequate in itself to explain the almost complete triumph of evil. The Gentile world, totally submerged in idolatry and immorality, had nevertheless been victorious over the people of God. Many Jews had denied their ancestral faith and chosen to live like Gentiles. In spite of this they had prospered. The saving knowledge of the true God was held by only a small and despised minority of mankind. The persistent and growing success of evil seemed more than human. There must be a demonic supernatural power, which had set itself against the true God and built for itself a kingdom of evil.

There were in the Old Testament indications of such superhuman evil powers: the serpent who tempted Eve (Gen. 3:1); the sons of God who by sexual intercourse with human women spawned a race of giants (ch. 6:1-4); the demons of the desert and of the night occasionally mentioned in Old Testament books (Lev. 17:7; Ps. 106:37; Isa. 34:14); and the Satan (literally, "the Adversary") who tormented Job and accused Joshua before the Lord (Job 1:6; Zech. 3:1). The Persian religion, with which the Jews were in contact from the time of the exile, was the principal outside influence contributing to the idea of cosmic evil. It saw reality in terms of a struggle between two spiritual powers, symbolized by light and darkness. The powers of darkness and evil were ruled by a demonic prince, Angra Mainyu, who with his hosts of evil spirits fought perpetually against the forces of light and goodness, controlled by Ahura Mazda and his seven archangels. The varying fortunes of the battle determined the course of human history, and would continue to do so until the forces of evil were conquered and destroyed.

Inter-Testamental Judaism borrowed a good deal from the Persian religion. The leader of the spiritual hosts of evil was known by several different names: Mastema (the Enemy), Semjaza, Azazel (see Lev. 16:8), Belial (in the Dead Sea scrolls), Beliar (in The Testaments of the Twelve Patriarchs), Satan, and the devil. He commanded a host of malicious demons who tempted human beings to lies, deceit, fornication, murder, and blasphemy. In their role as tempters the demons were only following their leader, for it was he who took the form of a serpent and led Eve astray. The demons are the gods of the pagan nations.

Judaism could not, however, go all the way with Persian religion. It did not doubt the reality and efficiency of the evil spirits, but it could not permit their existence to threaten the universal sovereignty of God. The demons existed by his permission, they continued by his sufferance, and they would cease at his command. There is no genuine cosmic dualism in Jewish thought.

Demonology is a heady subject that stirs up the imagination and sometimes makes it run wild. Space permits mention of only two out of the fascinating variety of demonologies that flourished on the threshold of Christianity. The Manual of Discipline of the Qumrân community asserts the sovereignty of God over both angels and demons. " He created the spirits of light and of darkness, and upon them he founded every work " (iv. 25). But their origins are different. One comes from " the abode of light "; and other from " the well of darkness " (iv. 18, 19). " In the hand of the angel of darkness is all dominion over the sons of error " (iv. 20, 21), and " in the hand of the prince of lights is dominion over all the sons of righteousness " (iv. 20). The present age is " the dominion of Belial " (the angel of darkness). The demonology of I Enoch, which resembles that of Jubilees, is more complex. Satan, one of the archangels, seduced a group of angels called " the Watchers " to rebel against God. Conquered and cast out of heaven, Satan took revenge by tempting Eve to disobey God. The Watchers, banished to earth, were given the task of instructing the human race. Instead, they fell in love with human women and fathered a race of giants. God, angered by their deeds, imprisoned the Watchers in the earth, killed the giants, and destroyed corrupt mankind by the flood. But the souls of the giants released at their death, became demons, and under the command of Satan continued their attacks on mankind. (I Enoch, chs. 6 to 11.) Presumably the amorous demon of the book of Tobit, who loved Sarah and killed all her husbands on their wedding night, was one of these (Tobit 6:13-14).

The point of importance about demonology is not its bizarre and lurid details. It reflects a deep conviction of the seriousness of evil. The battle that goes on between good and evil within every human being is only one small episode in a universal contest between right and wrong, which reaches even to the heavenly places and engages God himself. The letter to the Ephesians shares this conviction: "We are not contending against flesh and blood, but against the principalities, against the powers, against the world rulers of this present darkness, against the spiritual hosts of wickedness in the heavenly places." (Ch. 6:12.)

Who Are God's Allies?

The God of the Old Testament is often pictured as a monarch surrounded by a heavenly court that carries out the orders of the divine King. Angels spoke to Abraham, Moses, Gideon, and others, and, when Jacob fell asleep at Bethel, he dreamed of a ladder stretching from heaven to earth with the messengers of God ascending and descending on it (Gen. 28:12). The Old Testament angels are featureless creatures without names or personalities. They are the voice, eyes, and hands of God on earth, and are little more than devices for explaining how the God who lives in heaven can be active in the world at a particular time and place.

The writers of the inter-Testamental period were reluctant to bring their transcendent God into too close contact with the fallen world, and, accordingly, they made increasing use of angel mediators to bridge the gulf between God and man. The Persian religion had a well-developed angelology, which served as a model for Jewish authors. The angels began to take on personalities of their own. Special functions were assigned to them, and they were given places in a heavenly organization. According to The Book of Jubilees, three classes of angels were formed on the first day of the Creation: the Angels of the Presence, the Angels of Sanctification, and the lesser angels who preside over such things as fire, wind, and clouds. (Ch. 2:1-2.) The most illustrious members of the heavenly host were the four (sometimes seven) archangels, whose names became household words. Michael, the guardian spirit of Israel, appears in the late chapters of Daniel (chs. 10:13, 21; 12:1). Raphael became the traveling companion and guard of the young man Tobias (Tobit, ch. 5). Uriel warned Noah of the impending flood (I Enoch 10:1). Gabriel interpreted Daniel's dreams (Dan. 8:16; 9:21) and announced the coming birth of Jesus (Luke 1:19). These actions are typical of the mediating function of the angels, who do God's bidding on earth, carry God's word to men, bring the prayers of the devout into the presence of God, guard and protect faithful men, and combat the demonic forces of Satan.

The inter-Testamental tendency to personify, which we observed in the case of the angels, operated also on wisdom and the law. The divine Wisdom was described as a woman " more beautiful than the sun " (Wisd. of Sol. 7:29), " a reflection of eternal light . . . and an image of his goodness " (v. 26; compare the description of Christ in Col. 1:15-20). A significant passage in The Wisdom of Solomon presents human history from Adam to Moses as guided by the saving activity of Wisdom (chs. 10 and 11). Wisdom is one of God's most potent allies, for against her "evil does not prevail" (ch. 7:30). The will of God, embodied in the law, was also personified, and was for all practical purposes identified with Wisdom (Ecclus. 15:1; 21:11; 34:8). Although revealed in time, the law was timeless and eternal (II Esdras 9:37; The Book of Jubilees 33:17). It was the true source of light and life (II Baruch 18:1; 38:2).

Righteous men, not in isolation but *as members of a righteous community,* are God's human allies. They are the foot-slogging infantry soldiers on the firing line of the battle, expendable, and likely to be hurt or killed. The devout Jew of the period would have identified himself at once with the spirit of the gospel song by P. P. Bliss:

> "See the mighty host advancing,
> Satan leading on:
> Mighty men around us falling,
> Courage almost gone!"

The faithful in Israel thought of themselves as a besieged strong point in an invaded country. Their duty was to hold the fort with patient endurance until God's reinforcements arrived and the Messianic Age dawned. It was a high calling and a dangerous one, demanding self-sacrificing courage; but in fulfilling it the man of faith felt himself to be, literally, on the side of the angels.

CHAPTER 6 | *The Age to Come*

THE science of physics makes a good deal of the laws of the conservation of matter and energy. Matter and energy may pass through many transformations, but, though the form may alter, nothing is lost or destroyed. A fair case could be made for a law of the conservation of values. The insights, ideals, and hopes that guided a nation in its historic past may be twisted by circumstances into radically new patterns, but the values contained in them will usually be stubbornly conserved. So it seems, at least, with the apocalyptic literature. Its visionary accounts of the future age—the dead starting from their graves, the heavenly hosts, the supernatural Messiah, the New Jerusalem descending majestically from heaven like a giant visitor from outer space, the flaming pit of torment, and the eternal delights of paradise where people live for a thousand years and feast on heavenly manna—these come strangely into a modern world of steel and concrete. But we have to realize that these symbols represent serious attempts by hard-pressed men to preserve the values of Israel's religious heritage at a time when the events of history threatened it with destruction.

In weird and fantastic forms, the visions of the age to come asserted the eternal validity of five basic concepts of Old Testament faith. (1) This faith rested on the identity of *Israel as the covenant community,* chosen by the grace of God and destined for a position of world-wide influence. But that community was now scattered abroad and divided at home (see Chapters 2 and 3). (2) God's unbreakable promise had given his nation *the holy soil of Palestine* for a homeland *and the sacred hill of Zion* as a capital city and place of worship forever. Over both of these the heathen now ruled. (3) The Lord had established his *covenant with David* that a king of Davidic descent would reign forever over the chosen people. In spite of the promise of God, the Davidic succession had been broken. (4) On the theological side *God's creative power,* by which he had formed the universe and called it good, was challenged by an intrusion of evil into the creation on such a scale as to corrupt it through and through. (5) Similarly, *the justice of God,* which demanded that goodness be rewarded and evil punished, did not seem to work in a world that crowned evil with success and killed the saints. The inter-Testamental theologian had the herculean task of maintaining these articles of faith in the face of facts, and it is small wonder that he strained language trying to accomplish it.

Human beings are incurably hopeful, and when they have no ground for hope in the present they invariably look to the future for better days ahead. The apocalyptists went farther. They looked, not to the future as something that grows out of the present, but beyond the future and beyond time itself. They believed that for their ideals to be realized the present depraved order must come to a complete end and be replaced by a totally different order, contrasting in every respect with the present age. In apocalyptic thought the "now" and the "then" are separated by a yawning gulf, and hope lies exclusively on the other side. For many Jews on the threshold of Christianity, faith had come to mean faith in the age to come.

Because no one has experienced the opposite of the present age, the only language that can be used of it is the language of symbolic imagery. In order to express the *complete* opposite of this age, the imagery is heightened, strained, and distorted. Lacking the control of actual experience, descriptions of the age to come necessarily depend on speculation and imagination, and hence no uniformity can be expected among them. The visionary literature of the inter-Testamental period displays just such a rich variety of vivid but inconsistent, fantastic, and impossible imagery.

The reader may check the accuracy of these introductory paragraphs by examining Dan., chs. 11 and 12; II Esdras, chs. 11 to 13; I Enoch, ch. 90; The Psalms of Solomon, ch. 17; II Baruch, chs. 29 and 30, and by looking again at the great New Testament apocalypse, the book of Revelation.

The Apocalyptic Pattern

The shape of things to come in its simplest form is a contrast of two ages, the one corrupt and the other glorious (Tobit 14:1-8). Daniel 12:1-3 expands the pattern by introducing the resurrection of the dead at the transition between the ages. "There shall be a time of trouble; . . . but at that time your people shall be delivered. . . . And many of those who sleep in the dust of the earth shall awake. . . . And those who are wise shall shine like the brightness of the firmament." More highly developed descriptions of the future age elaborate and complicate the idea further. Although the variations found in apocalyptic literature are almost as numerous as the writers, five elements are nearly always found in a fixed order, and these constitute, as it were, the basic pattern of apocalyptic.

1. The coming of the Messiah.
2. The work of the Messiah.
3. The resurrection of the dead.

4. The Last Judgment.
5. The glorious age of the Kingdom of God.

Darkness Before Dawn

The present age, sinking deeper and deeper into the quicksand of evil, should logically end by disappearing altogether beneath its slimy surface. The time of confusion and disorder at the end of the age, when all the devils of hell will be let loose to torment the world (Rev. 9:7-11), is described with evident relish in the apocalypses. In II Baruch, for example, the twelve phases of the end include such horrors as fire, earthquake, famine, plague, and war. The whole of nature is caught up in the turmoil: stones speak, wooden beams drip blood, stars fall to earth, and mysterious figures sweep the heavens (II Esdras 5:1-13). Christians know the period of tribulations better from the descriptions of them in the " Little Apocalypse " of Mark, ch. 13, and the " three woes " of Rev., chs. 9 to 12. According to the apocalyptists, *when man tries to rule his own destiny without reference to God, the end result is the shambles of a crumbled world:* " If the Lord had not shortened the days, no human being would be saved " (Mark 13:20). But in man's last extremity, God acts to save the righteous, and the Messianic Age begins to emerge.

Stubborn logic, as well as overheated imagination, is at work in the descriptions of the " woes " before the end of the age. Since the same God who made the world at the beginning will remake it at the end, his first act and his last will resemble each other. In the beginning he found " waste and void " and by his word he transformed the chaos into an ordered universe. Evil, human and superhuman, had turned the Creation back to chaos, and the bleeding sticks and talking stones of apocalyptic imagery are intended to emphasize the complete chaos that will precede the new creation.

The principle that the end of time resembles its beginning was a fundamental one for inter-Testamental thought. We shall see it operating in every aspect of the future age. It helped, for example, to shape some of the answers to the inevitable question, When will the end come? One of these answers was logical. The creation had lasted six days, and a day in God's sight is as a thousand years. The world should, therefore, have a corresponding life span of six thousand years. A second answer was numerical. At the Creation, God had fixed the number of human beings (or of righteous human beings) who were to be born. When the quota was filled the end would come. A third answer was ethical. The law was created to guide the life of Israel, and if the nation observed it perfectly for a single day, the Messiah would appear.

The Coming of the Messiah

Although exceedingly important, the Messiah is not absolutely necessary to apocalyptic thought. God may himself bring in the New Age, and rule it in his own person without viceroy or intermediary. When the Messiah does figure in an apocalyptic book, he stands like a bridge between the two ages. He comes in the last phase of the present age, and his rule may carry over into the age to come. He is, in fact, the instrument of God for transforming the one into the other. His appearance is not, however, unannounced. Moses, Elijah, or some other member of the prophetic line was expected to precede the Messiah to prepare the way for him, proclaiming him publicly to the people, and anointing him as the prophets had anointed the kings of old. The Christian church took over this pattern of thought to explain the relationship of John the Baptist, the second Elijah, to Jesus Christ, the Savior Messiah.

The concept of the messiah is historically and intellectually derived from the institution of kingship. Theologically it rests on the covenant between God and David, which guaranteed Israel a Davidic king in perpetuity. Thus, in its simplest form, messianic thought requires only that in the coming age an unbroken dynasty of Davidic kings should rule over restored Israel. Simplicity was not, however, the strong point of inter-Testamental thought. The more otherworldly the future age became, the more the Messiah was pictured in superhuman terms. The line of Davidic kings was reduced to a single figure, sinless and eternal, who would rule forever in the new age. The nature of this timeless man became the subject of much speculation. Some believed that God had created him before the world, and had kept him in the heavenly places until it was time for him to be born in the family of David, or to appear on the clouds of heaven and begin his delivering work.

Inter-Testamental literature has an imposing list of titles suited to the divine origin and exalted rank of the supernatural Messiah, many of which the New Testament adopted and applied to Christ; for example, the Righteous One (I Enoch 53:6; Acts 3:14), the Elect One (I Enoch 40:5; Luke 9:35), the Son of David (II Esdras 12:32; Mark 10:47), the Son of Man (I Enoch 46:2-3; Mark 9:9, 12, 31), and the Son of God (II Esdras 7:28; Rom. 1:4).

Two of the messianic names need a brief explanation. " Son of God " is a very old title used both for the Israelite monarch (Ps. 2:7) and the angels (Job 2:1). Its double connotation, linking together divinity and kingship, and its suggestion of a peculiarly intimate relationship with God make it a perfect messianic name. " Son of man," used in Dan. 7:13, refers to an empire, not to an individual. Daniel dreamed of four ferocious beasts: a winged lion, a bear, a four-winged leopard, and an indescribable creature with iron teeth. Each beast represented one of the bestial and brutal world empires. After them a fifth empire of divine origin (it came on the clouds of heaven), called the " Saints of the Most High," appeared. In contrast to its bestial forerunners, this empire was represented by a human figure, " one like a son of man." This title had the right note of mystery to qualify it as a messianic name, and I Enoch applied it to the supernatural Messiah.

Exodus 40:15 says of the sons of Aaron: " Their anointing shall admit them to a perpetual priesthood throughout their generations." This anointing to an everlasting covenant was an open invitation to think of the chief priest as a messianic figure analogous to the Davidic king, especially since in the Greek period the ruling priest had been the real political power in Judea (see Chapter 2). The Testaments of the Twelve Patriarchs looked for a Messiah of the tribe of Levi, and the priestly-minded Dead Sea sect expected that in the age to come a high priest would share the rule of restored Israel with the royal Messiah, and would, in fact, be the more important of the two. The Manual of Discipline sums up in one sentence the whole range of messianic thought with which we have been dealing: " There shall arise a prophet and the Messiahs of Aaron and Israel."

The Work of the Messiah

Variety is not lacking in inter-Testamental accounts of the work of the Messiah, but in all of them his mighty acts are directed to the same end. He will establish Israel for all time as the covenant community, living under God's rule on the sacred soil of Palestine, and he will carry out Israel's redeeming mission to the nations of the world. The short description that follows is frankly artificial. It cannot capture the additions, omissions, changes in order, and shifts of emphasis of the documents themselves, and it can give only a pale impression of a hope that was once powerful enough to sustain the armies of Bar-Cochba in three years of hopeless warfare against the might of Rome (see Chapter 2).

When the Messiah appears his enemies will muster for a decisive battle against the people of God, led by the menacing figure of an antimessiah (the "last leader" of II Baruch 40:1), who, like Gog in Ezek., ch. 38, is dedicated to the destruction of the godly. The Messiah will gather his own forces to meet this last upsurge of paganism, and he will destroy his enemies by force of arms (as in the Dead Sea War scroll), or will melt them like snow by the word of his mouth (II Esdras, ch. 13). The earthly warfare is paralleled by a superhuman struggle in which the angels of light overthrow, bind, and imprison the demonic forces of the universe (I Enoch, ch. 10). After the victory, Jerusalem will be restored by purification of the earthly city (The Psalms of Solomon 17; 23; 33; Tobit 14:5) or by the descent from heaven of a glorious New Jerusalem (II Esdras 10:45-49; I Enoch 90:28-29; see Rev., ch. 21).

The Messiah's work now enters its final phase. He gathers the scattered people from the lands to which they have been dispersed and unites them into one community of the faithful. (II Esdras 13:39-47.) The dead are not forgotten, for the righteous who died without seeing the triumph of God pass through the resurrection and the judgment into the new life. The worthy Gentiles who survive "the woes" and who do not ally themselves with the antimessiah will "turn to fear the Lord God in truth, and will bury their idols" (Tobit 14:6).

The world has now been restored in conformity to the plan of God. Although the Messiah rules the new order from the city of Jerusalem, "he does none of these things by his own will but in obedience to the good ordinances of the mighty God" (The Sibylline Oracles 3:655-656). The real rule belongs to God, and the Kingdom is properly called "the Kingdom of Heaven." There is no more sickness, disease, want, discord, war, or evil, but eternal joy, prosperity, and peace (II Baruch, chs. 29 and 30; see Rev. 7:13-17). The long historical process that began when Israel accepted the covenant at Sinai has now, in spite of many checks and disasters, reached its appointed end.

The Resurrection Hope

If the Messiah belongs essentially to the age to come, and rules eternally over a transformed world, the resurrection and the Last Judgment must take place during the Messianic Era. But to some, who wished to make the gulf between this age and the next as wide and as deep as possible, the idea of an endless rule of the Messiah on earth was not nearly drastic enough. It looked too much like a continuation on a somewhat higher level of the present historic structure, and their faith would be satisfied with nothing less than a new creation. They tended, therefore, to think of the Messiah and his work as the closing phase of the present age, and to look beyond him to a still more glorious future.

Second Esdras made the cleavage between the two ages as sharp as a sword stroke.

> " My son the Messiah shall be revealed with those who are with him, and those who remain shall rejoice four hundred years [compare the thousand-year reign of the Messiah in Rev. 20:1-7]. And after these years my son the Messiah shall die, and all who draw human breath. And the world shall be turned back to primeval silence for seven days, as it was at the first beginnings; so that no one shall be left. And after seven days the world, which is not yet awake, shall be roused, and that which is corruptible shall perish. And the earth shall give up

> those who are asleep in it; . . . and the chambers shall give up the souls which have been committed to them." (Ch. 7:28-32.)

In New Testament times the Sadducees denied the resurrection. Greek thought influenced some Jews, particularly those living in Egypt, to believe in the immortality of the soul, an idea that found noble poetic expression in The Wisdom of Solomon.

> " The souls of the righteous are in the hand of God. . . .
> In the eyes of the foolish they seem to have died, . . .
> And their going from us to be their destruction;
> but they are at peace."
>
> (Ch. 3:1-4.)

The Pharisees, and with them most of the common people, attached their faith to the resurrection of the body at the Last Day. Jesus agreed with the Pharisees against the Sadducees, and the resurrection of the body passed over into Christian doctrine and found a permanent home in the last sentence of the Apostles' Creed.

In spite of its being in Christianity from the beginning, not all Christians are entirely comfortable with the doctrine of bodily resurrection. It suggests mutilated and disfigured corpses starting up out of their graves at the sound of the last trumpet, and we are apt to dismiss it as " too materialistic." The believer of the inter-Testamental period, however, regarded it as the inevitable consequence of the Biblical doctrine of Creation. The martyrs in II Maccabees — scalped, disemboweled, and shorn of hands and feet — confidently expected to receive these organs back at the resurrection, not by mechanical reassembling of the scattered parts, but by the creative activity of God (ch. 7:23). When God created Adam he molded a body and breathed into it the breath of life. God is concerned with the whole man, not with a fraction or fragment of human nature. Accordingly, the human being, recreated at the resurrection, must also possess a body, animated by the breath of God. Since the man who dies and the man who is raised are the same personality, the resurrection body must in a sense be the same as the earthly body (II Baruch 50:3-4), but only in a sense. The resurrection body is changed, glorified, incorruptible, everlasting, and purged of weakness, sinfulness, and subjection to death (II Baruch 51:10; I Cor. 15:37-50).

Ideas, like people, have a parentage and a family history. One of the ancestors of the resurrection of the body is the Old Testament conception of Sheol. At death the body decayed in the grave, but a shade of the dead man—not a soul, but something like the popular idea of a ghost—went to the underworld region, called " Sheol," where it continued a helpless and hopeless existence that can be called survival but not life. Too weak to disturb the dust, the shades of the good and the evil mingled together in the land of no return. The Israelite of Biblical times looked for his effective immortality in the family. If sons bearing his name continued within the covenant community, he had all the immortality he expected, and he could sleep in peace " with his fathers," knowing that his name was kept in remembrance.

The Israelite of Old Testament times also believed that God rewarded the nation for obedience and punished her for rebellion. When, after the exile, the individual became increasingly important in religious thought, this was taken to mean that God would reward his faithful servants and punish apostates and pagans individually. If he is a God of justice and loving-kindness, he will not simply discard like worn-out garments those who have been faithful to him through peril and trial, but will raise them to share in the age to come. Put in these terms the doctrine of the resurrection became a theological necessity.

Interest in the fate of the individual after death did not altogether obscure the traditional concern for Israel as the covenant community. The individual was raised that he might take his place, side by side with the great heroes of the past, in an Israel restored, redeemed, and glorified.

Judgment and Renewal

The resurrection is the necessary prelude to the Day of Judgment. In some apocalypses the judgment is implied in the resurrection itself. Only the good are raised; the wicked are left to the eternal extinction of death. Usually the judgment is more dramatic than this. The wicked and the righteous rise together. God appears on his throne of judgment, and the heavenly books recording the deeds of men are opened. Now mercy ceases, and justice, not blind but with sword in hand, stands alone. The wicked are condemned to the " pit of torment " in the black recesses of hell, and the righteous enter the " paradise of delight " (II Esdras 7:35-36).

This paradise of delight is often an earthly paradise, where all the injustices of the evil age are removed (The Testament of Judah 25:4), and the redeemed enjoy perpetual sunshine and peace (The Sibylline Oracles 4:190-191). Other writers speak of a paradise beyond time and in another world. After the judgment the righteous will pass through a series of transformations from beauty to loveliness and from light to glory, until they are able to see a land hitherto invisible to them. Here they associate with the angels and see the living creatures around the throne of God. After witnessing the glorification of the righteous, the wicked also are transformed. Their appearance becomes ugly in conformity with their evil natures, and they waste away in eternal punishment (II Baruch, ch. 51; see II Enoch 65:8-10; Rev. 7:14-17).

Because it seemed hard that the righteous should have to linger in the darkness of the underworld until Judgment Day, apocalyptic imagination transformed Sheol into a combination of heaven and hell under one roof. The righteous waited in a place of light and joy for their final release. Unpunished sinners were confined in a place of suffering until the resurrection, when they would be condemned to further pains. Sinners who had been punished in life inhabited a neutral region. They would not be raised or punished further (I Enoch, ch. 22).

The two preceding chapters have attempted to give a fair picture of the visionary world of apocalyptic, and at the same time to show that the writers were in their own way defending the basic tenets of their faith and trying to make them relevant to the extremely disheartening age in which they lived. Their work created a world view that dominated the minds of the Gospel writers, as the language and ideas of scientific technology often dominate our own.

CHAPTER 7 | *Life Under the Law*

WORKS AND FAITH

FOR the Jew of the first century before Christ, salvation meant to have a share in the age to come, but the present life could not be shrugged off as an unimportant episode on the road to glory. How a man stood on Judgment Day depended on his performance, measured by the twofold standard of trust and obedience, faith and works. Although a sectarian group like the Dead Sea community might alter the formula to include its beloved teacher, and expect salvation "because of their labor and faith in the teacher of righteousness" (The Habakkuk Commentary), for the majority the requirement of God was unbending allegiance to himself and absolute obedience to his will as expressed in the law.

Rules that seem to be entirely mechanical or ritualistic were to the Jew the marks that distinguished the covenant people from the pagan world. Circumcision on the eighth day, meticulous observance of the many regulations governing the Sabbath, dietary restrictions, ritual washings, tithes and offerings, prescribed periods of fasting, and long, expensive trips to Jerusalem for the great yearly festivals were the badges and visible signs of the Jewish community.

It is unfair to think of Judaism as completely bound up in

the external and ritualistic. It aimed at creating a communal life, healthy and acceptable to God. Recognizing the family as the fundamental unit of society, it insisted on purity in the marriage relationship and honor to parents. Although stern parental discipline was expected ("He who loves his son will whip him often," Ecclus. 30:1), affection and loyalty were the real heart of Jewish family life. In wider community relations honesty in the market place and impartial justice in the law courts were demanded, without neglect of the kindlier virtues of forgiveness and love. There is a New Testament ring to the instruction of The Testament of Dan:

"Love the Lord through all your life,
And one another with a true heart."
(Ch. 5:3.)

Care for the poor and needy was the best of good deeds, most acceptable to God because it so resembled his own character, "helper of the oppressed, upholder of the weak, . . . savior of those without hope" (Judith 9:11).

It must be admitted that this code of social behavior did not always extend to foreigners. Trickery and violence were applauded if they were used against the enemies of God (as in Judith). Most Jews, however, were content to live peaceably in the Gentile world, and to leave vengeance until the Day of the Lord. Education was valued as a means of getting on in the world, especially by those who followed the tradition of the Old Testament wisdom writers, but manual labor was by no means despised. After pointing out that laborers are not much sought after to fill high and responsible offices, Ecclesiasticus concludes:

"But they keep stable the fabric of the world,
and their prayer is in the practice of their trade."
(Ch. 38:34.)

Inter-Testamental Judaism was a religion of the heart as well as of rituals and of social ethics. The literature everywhere emphasizes the necessity of humility and repentance. Pride is the ugliest manifestation of human sin and calls down the stern judgment of God (Judith 9:9). The inwardness of inter-Testamental religion is nowhere so well revealed as in the prayers with which the literature abounds. Daniel preferred death in a den of lions to abandoning his practice of prayer three times a day with his face toward Jerusalem (Dan., ch. 6). These prayers are usually modeled on the Biblical psalms, and they contain a strong and moving element of adoration of God's majesty and power, united with a sense of the complete dependence of the worshiper on his love and mercy (see, for example, Tobit 8:5-6, 14-17).

Attitudes to the Law

The deathbed speech, attributed in I Maccabees to Mattathias, the initiator of the Maccabean Revolt, begins with these words: " Arrogance and reproach have now become strong; it is a time of ruin and furious anger. Now, my children, *show zeal for the law, and give your lives for the covenant of our fathers* " (ch. 2:49-50). Men cannot be brought to die for anything that they do not believe to be worth living for. The Torah had in the postexilic period stepped out of relative obscurity to take the center of the religious stage. It was the object of study, of devotion, and of self-sacrifice. Imperishable, unique, and holy, the law was the lamp that guided the faithful in the way of peace, and the rallying point around which they gathered for war.

There were those, of course, to whom the minute details of the law were a burden, which they either refused to acknowledge or to which they gave grudging obedience. There were also the sticklers, who took unholy delight in the minutiae of the law, and who held all who did not do so in contempt (Matt. 23:23). But many an Israelite loved the law as the gift of God to his nation, and obeyed its smallest detail gladly as part of the privilege of being within the covenant. Christians, seeing the law through the eyes of Paul, are often led to believe that it was a sterile thing without spiritual power. But this view of the law leaves us unable to account for the fact that the gospel made relatively little headway among the Jews of the first century. They felt that under the law they already possessed true liberty and did not need the freedom offered them in the gospel.

The House of Prayer

A first-century visitor to the Jewish quarter of any Roman city would have observed that the community center was a building that served as school, town hall, distributing center for aid to the needy, and place of worship. In its main hall the seven-branched lampstand suggested the Jerusalem Temple, but the place of honor was given to the books of the law. The institution was not controlled by a priestly group but by an elected council of elders, who managed its business affairs and supervised its worship. At the informal services conducted by laymen, the congregation sat in groups according to their trades, to be led in prayer and to hear the law read and explained. They had the opportunity to join in the responses and to discuss the interpretation of the law to which they had listened.

This unique institution, the synagogue, was the child of the inter-Testamental period, born of reverence for the law, and of the desire to worship the God of Israel in areas remote from the Jerusalem Temple. The Holy City, the Temple, the altar, the daily sacrifices, and the ordained priesthood occupied a high place in the affections of the Jewish people until, with the first revolt against Rome, they ceased to operate as living institutions and became a memory and a hope for the future. But the synagogue, not tied to any sacred place but established wherever there was a community of believing Jews, outlived the destruction of the Temple, and it has carried the religion of the law across twenty centuries to the present day.

~

In our brief survey of the four centuries of struggle and turmoil, from the conquest of the East by Alexander the Great to the last valiant but ill-starred revolt of the Jewish people against the Roman power, we have been witnesses of the end of an era. The firm line of tradition that began at Sinai and was preserved by the heroic labors of the prophets is broken in violence and confusion, sectarianism and war. But as the splendor fades away something new comes into existence. The end is also the beginning or, rather, two separate beginnings.

The young Christian churches, now cut off from their place of origin in Palestine, face the Gentile world, interpret their gospel in the language of its philosophies, and eventually conquer it and become recognized as the religion of the state. The Jewish faith, disappointed in its hope of military victory in the Messianic Age, turns to the law and the synagogue. Generations of devoted scholars produce that monumental interpretation of the law, the Talmud, which forms the basis of present-day Judaism, and make the synagogue the instrument par excellence for the teaching of the law. We have seen in these pages the breaking of the Old Testament tradition and the promise of its two legitimate successors, rabbinic Judaism and modern Christianity.